You Can't
Be Neutral
on a
Moving Train

Howard Zinn

You Can't Be Neutral on a Moving Train

A Personal History of Our Times

Beacon Press
BOSTON

To Roslyn,
for everything

BEACON PRESS
25 Beacon Street
Boston, Massachusetts 02108-2892

Beacon Press books are published under the auspices
of the Unitarian Universalist Association of Congregations.

09 08   10 9 8 7

Text design by Daniel Ochsner
Composition by Wilsted & Taylor

Library of Congress Cataloging-in-Publication Data

Zinn, Howard.
    You can't be neutral on a moving train : a personal history of our times /
Howard Zinn.
        p.   cm.
    Includes index.
    ISBN 0-8070-7058-0 (cloth)
    ISBN 0-8070-7127-7 (paper)
        1. Zinn, Howard, [date].   2. Historians—United States—Biography.
    3. United States—History—1945–   —Philosophy.   I. Title.
    E175.5.Z25A3   1994
    973'.07202—dc20   94-8000

CONTENTS

It has been eight years since this memoir was first published, and as I write now, the nation is in a state of great tension. On September 11, 2001, teams of hijackers flew two passenger planes, loaded with jet fuel, into the twin towers of the World Trade Center in downtown Manhattan, and the ensuing catastrophe killed close to three thousand people who were burned or crushed to death as the buildings burst into flames and collapsed.

Like so many others who saw those events on television, I was horrified. And when President George W. Bush immediately announced to the nation that we were now at war, I was horrified again because solving problems with bombs has never worked. It seemed clear to me that this was exactly the wrong response to the act of terrorism that had just occurred. And when, soon after, the United States began bombing Afghanistan, I considered that, if terrorism can be defined as the willingness to kill innocent people for some presumed good cause, this was another form of terrorism— one I had seen up close many years ago after meeting the survivors of Hiroshima and Nagasaki who also suffered needlessly for an alleged "good cause."

In this book I tell of my experience as a bombardier in the Second World War. I describe how I came to the conclusion, after dropping bombs on European cities, and celebrating the victory over fascism, that war, even a "good war," while it may bring immediate relief, cannot solve fundamental problems. Indeed, the glow of that "good war" has been used to cast a favorable light over every bad war for the next fifty years, wars in which our government lied to us, and millions of innocent people died.

Just five years after the end of the Second World War, we were at war with Korea, bombing villages, using napalm, destroying much of the country. That war was barely over when the United States intervened in Vietnam, with a half million troops and the most deadly bombing campaign in world history. I write here about my involvement in the movement against that war. Since then, our government has found reasons to bomb Panama, and Iraq, and Yugoslavia. We have become addicted to war.

Today the movie screens are filled with images of military heroism, and my generation is hailed as "the greatest generation." In such films as *Band of Brothers, Windtalkers, Saving Private Ryan, Memphis Belle,* and others, World War II is being brought back to make us feel good about war.

My refusal to justify war has a simple logic. War in our time inevitably means the indiscriminate killing of large numbers of innocent people (no matter what claims are made by confident government officials about "smart bombs" and "we only aim at military targets"). Thus, the means of waging war are evil and certain. The ends of war, however proclaimed as noble (putting aside the historical evidence that aims are not really "democracy" and "liberty," but political ambition, corporate profit, a lust for oil), are always uncertain.

Two months after the United States began to bomb Afghanistan, I read a dispatch by a reporter for the *Boston Globe,* writing from a hospital in Jalalabad. "In one bed lay Noor Mohammad, 10, who was a bundle of bandages. He lost his eyes and hands to the bomb that hit his house after Sunday dinner. . . . The hospital's morgue received 17 bodies last weekend, and officials here estimate at least 89 civilians were killed in several villages."

The moral question was clear. One boy now without hands and eyes. There was no possible connection between him and the events of September 11 in New York. There was no possibility that the crippling of his face and body, or that any of the bombs dropped for months on Afghanistan, would reduce or eliminate terrorism. Indeed, more likely, the acts of violence on both sides would reinforce one another, and would create an endless cycle of death and suffering.

That scene in the hospital would need to be multiplied by a thousand times (because at least a thousand, and perhaps five thousand civilians died under our bombs, with many others maimed, wounded) to make a proper moral reckoning of whether the war on Afghanistan can be justified by anyone claiming to care about human rights.

I write this book about "growing up class-conscious." As I look around at the world in 2002, I am even more aware today that behind the deceptive words designed to entice people into supporting violence—words like *democracy, freedom, self-defense, national security*—there is the reality of enormous wealth in the hands of a few, while billions of people in the world are hungry, sick, homeless. President Eisenhower, himself a warrior, in one of his better moments, called the billions spent on preparations for war "a theft" from those who are without food, without shelter.

There is a sense of desperation and helplessness in the land. There is the feel of a country occupied by a foreign power, not foreign in the sense of coming from abroad, but rather foreign to the principles we want our country to stand for. The "war on terror" is being used to create an atmosphere of hysteria, in which the claim of "national security" becomes an excuse to throw aside the guarantees of the Bill of Rights, to give new powers to the FBI. The question not asked is whether the war itself creates great dangers for the security of the American people, and also for the security of innocent people abroad, who become pawns in the game to expand American power worldwide.

I write in this book about law and justice, about prisons and courts—and we have more prisons than ever before, and the courts still pretend to "equal justice." It is the poor, the nonwhite, the nonconformists, the powerless who go to prison while corporate thieves and government architects of war remain at large.

Considering all this, I might be incurably depressed, except for other experiences—exhilarating, inspiring—that I write about in this book. The early chapters deal with my seven years in the South, when my wife and children and I lived in the black community around Spelman College in Atlanta, and became participants in the southern movement for racial justice.

What did I learn? That small acts of resistance to authority, if persisted in, may lead to large social movements. That ordinary people are capable of extraordinary acts of courage. That those in power who confidently say "never" to the possibility of change may live to be embarrassed by those words. That the world of social struggle is full of surprises, as the common moral sense of people germinates invisibly, bubbles up, and at certain points in history brings about victories that may be small, but carry large promise.

Perhaps the most important thing I learned was about democracy, that democracy is not our government, our constitution, our legal structure. Too often they are enemies of democracy. Certainly this was the experience of African-Americans in this country for two hundred years. With the government failing to enforce the Fourteenth and Fifteenth Amendments to the Constitution, black men, women, and children decided to do that on their own. They organized, demonstrated, protested, challenged the law, were beaten, went to prison, some killed—and thereby reached the conscience of the nation and the world. And things changed. That's when democracy comes alive.

This book begins with an introduction subtitled "The Question Period in Kalamazoo." Since then, I have spoken hundreds of times all over the country to audiences ranging from several hundred to several thousand, to universities, high schools, community groups. Everywhere I went—whether in Columbia, Missouri, or Texas City, Texas; Oshkosh, Wisconsin, or Boulder, Colorado; Athens, Georgia, Manhattan, Kansas, Portland, Oregon, or Arcata, California—I encountered people who were determined to live in a just and peaceful world. They would resist war and hatred. They would bring democracy alive.

I hope this book, telling the stories of people I have known and loved, will be as encouraging to readers as it has been to me.

Perhaps the most important thing I learned was the meaning of democracy.

The Question Period
in Kalamazoo

I had been invited to give a talk in Kalamazoo, Michigan. It was the night of the final televised presidential debate of the 1992 campaign, and to my surprise (did they need a break from election madness?) there were several hundred people in the audience. This was the quincentennial year of the Columbus landing in the Western Hemisphere and I was speaking on "The Legacy of Columbus, 1492–1992."

Ten years earlier, in the very first pages of my book *A People's History of the United States*, I had written about Columbus in a way that startled readers. They, like me, had learned in elementary school (an account never contradicted, however far their education continued) that Columbus was one of the great heroes of world history, to be admired for his daring feat of imagination and courage. In my account, I acknowledged that he was an intrepid sailor, but also pointed out (based on his own journal and the reports of many eyewitnesses) that he was vicious in his treatment of the gentle Arawak Indians who greeted his arrival in this hemisphere. He enslaved them, tortured them, murdered them—all in the pursuit of wealth. He represented, I suggested, the worst values of Western civilization: greed, violence, exploitation, racism, conquest, hypocrisy (he claimed to be a devout Christian).

The success of *A People's History* took both me and my publisher by surprise. In its first decade it went through twenty-four printings, sold three hundred thousand copies, was nominated for an American Book Award, and was published in Great Britain and Japan. I began to get letters from all over the country, and a large proportion of them were in excited reaction to my opening chapter on Columbus.

Most of the letters thanked me for telling an untold story. A few were skeptical and indignant. One high school student in Oregon, assigned my book by his teacher, wrote: "You've said that you have gained a lot of this information from Columbus' own journal. I am wondering if there is such a journal, and if so, why isn't it part of our history? Why isn't any of what you say in my history book?" A mother in California, looking into a copy of *A People's History* her daughter had brought home from school, became enraged and demanded that the school board investigate the teacher who used my book in her classes.

It became clear that the problem (yes, I represented a problem) was not just my irreverence toward Columbus, but my whole approach to American history. In *A People's History*, I insisted, as one reviewer put it, on "a reversal of perspective, a reshuffling of heroes and villains." The Founding Fathers were not just ingenious organizers of a new nation (though they certainly were that) but also rich white slaveholders, merchants, bondholders, fearful of lower-class rebellion, or as James Madison put it, of "an equal division of property." Our military heroes—Andrew Jackson, Theodore Roosevelt—were racists, Indian-killers, war-lovers, imperialists. Our most liberal presidents—Jefferson, Lincoln, Wilson, Roosevelt, Kennedy—were more concerned with political power and national aggrandizement than with the rights of nonwhite people.

My heroes were the farmers of Shays' Rebellion, the black abolitionists who violated the law to free their brothers and sisters, the people who went to prison for opposing World War I, the workers who went on strike against powerful corporations, defying police and militia, the Vietnam veterans who spoke out against the war, the women who demanded equality in all aspects of life.

There were historians and teachers of history who welcomed my book. A number of people, though, were upset; to them I was clearly out of order. If there were criminal penalties I might have been charged with "assault with a deadly weapon—a book," or "disorderly conduct—making unseemly noises in an exclusive club," or "trespassing—on the sacred domain of historiographical tradition."

To some people, not only was my book out of order, my whole life was out of order—there was something unpatriotic, subversive, dangerous, in my criticism of so much that went on in this society. During the Gulf War of 1991, I gave a talk to a high school assembly in Massachusetts, at a private school where the students came from affluent families and were said to be "95 percent in favor of the war." I spoke my mind and to my surprise got a great round of applause. But in a classroom afterward, in a meeting with a small group of the students, a girl who had been staring at me with obvious hostility throughout the discussion suddenly spoke up, her voice registering her anger: "Why do you *live* in this country?"

I felt a pang. It was a question I knew people often had, even when it went unspoken. It was the issue of *patriotism*, of loyalty to one's country, which arises again and again, whether someone is criticizing foreign policy, or evading military service, or refusing to pledge allegiance to the flag.

I tried to explain that my love was for the *country*, for the people, not for whatever government happened to be in power. To believe in democracy was to believe in the principles of the Declaration of Independence—that government is an artificial creation, established by the people to defend the equal right of everyone to life, liberty, and the pursuit of happiness. I interpreted "everyone" to include men, women, and children all over the world, who have a right to life not to be taken away by their own government or by ours.

When a government betrays those democratic principles, *it* is being unpatriotic. A love of democracy would then require opposing your government. It would require being "out of order."

The publication of *A People's History* led to requests from around the country for me to speak. And so there I was in Kalamazoo that evening in 1992, speaking about why telling the truth about Columbus is important for us today. I was really not interested in Columbus himself, but in the issues raised by his interaction with the native Americans: Is it possible for people, overcoming history, to live together with equality, with dignity, today?

At the end of my talk, someone asked a question which has been put to me many times in different ways. "Given the depressing news of what is happening in the world, you seem surprisingly optimistic. What gives you hope?"

I attempted an answer. I said I could understand being depressed by the state of the world, but the questioner had caught my mood accurately. To him and to others, mine seemed an absurdly cheerful approach to a violent and unjust world. But to me what is often disdained as romantic idealism, as wishful thinking, is justified if it prompts *action* to fulfill those wishes, to bring to life those ideals.

The willingness to undertake such action cannot be based on certainties, but on those possibilities glimpsed in a reading of history different from the customary painful recounting of human cruelties. In such a reading we can find not only war but resistance to war, not only injustice but rebellion against injustice, not only selfishness but self-sacrifice, not only silence in the face of tyranny but defiance, not only callousness but compassion.

Human beings show a broad spectrum of qualities, but it is the worst of these that are usually emphasized, and the result, too often, is to dishearten us, diminish our spirit. And yet, historically, that spirit refuses to surrender. History is full of instances where people, against enormous odds, have come together to struggle for liberty and justice, and have *won*—not often enough, of course, but enough to suggest how much more is possible.

The essential ingredients of these struggles for justice are human beings who, if only for a moment, if only while beset with fears, step out of line and do *something*, however small. And even the smallest, most unheroic of acts adds to the store of kindling that may be ignited by some surprising circumstance into tumultuous change.

Individual people are the necessary elements, and my life has been full of such people, ordinary and extraordinary, whose very existence has given me hope. Indeed, the people there in that audience in Kalamazoo, clearly concerned with the world beyond the election returns, were living proof of possibilities for change in this difficult world.

Though I didn't say so to my last questioner, I had met such people that evening, in that city. At dinner before my talk I was with the campus parish priest, a man built like a football linebacker, which in fact he had been years before. I asked him the question I often ask people I like: "How did you come by the peculiar ideas you now have?"

His was a one-word answer, the same given by so many: "Vietnam." To life-probing questions there seems so often to be a one-word answer: Auschwitz . . . Hungary . . . Attica. Vietnam. The priest had served there as a chaplain. His commanding officer was Colonel George Patton III. A true son of his father, Patton liked to talk of his soldiers as "darn good killers," hesitating to use the word "damn" but not the word "killers." Patton ordered the chaplain to carry a pistol while in the combat zone. The chaplain refused, and despite threats, continued to refuse. He came out of Vietnam against not just that war but all wars. And now he was traveling back and forth to El Salvador to help people struggling against death squads and poverty.

Also at dinner was a young teacher of sociology at Michigan State University. Raised in Ohio by working-class parents, he too had come to oppose the war in Vietnam. Now he taught criminology, doing research not about robbers and muggers, but about high crime, about government officials and corporate executives whose victims were not individuals but the whole of society.

It's remarkable how much history there is in any small group. There was also at our table a young woman, a recent university graduate, who was entering nursing school so that she could be of use to villagers in Central America. I envied her. As one of the many who write, speak, teach, practice law, preach, whose contribution to society is so indirect, so uncertain, I thought of those who give immediate help—the carpenters, the nurses, the farmers, the school bus drivers, the mothers. I remembered the Chilean poet Pablo Neruda, who wrote a poem about his lifelong wish that he could do something useful with his hands, that he could make a broom, just a broom.

I didn't say any of this to my last questioner in Kalamazoo. In fact, to really answer him I would have had to say much more about why I was so curiously hopeful in the face of the world as we know it. I would have had to go back over my life.

I would have to tell about going to work in a shipyard at the age of eighteen and spending three years working on the docks, in the cold and heat, amid deafening noise and poisonous fumes, building battleships and landing ships in the early years of the Second World War.

I would have to tell about enlisting in the Air Force at twenty-one, being trained as a bombardier, flying combat missions in Europe, and later asking myself troubling questions about what I had done in the war.

And about getting married, becoming a father, going to college under the G.I. Bill while loading trucks in a warehouse, with my wife working and our two children in a charity day-care center, and all of us living in a low-income housing project on the Lower East Side of Manhattan.

And about getting my Ph.D. from Columbia and my first real teaching job (I had a number of unreal teaching jobs), going to live and teach in a black community in the Deep South for seven years. And about the students at Spelman College who one day decided to climb over a symbolic and actual stone wall surrounding the campus to make history in the early years of the civil rights movement.

And about my experiences in that movement, in Atlanta, in Albany, Georgia, and Selma, Alabama, in Hattiesburg and Jackson and Greenwood, Mississippi.

I would have to tell about moving north to teach in Boston, and joining the protests against the war in Vietnam, and being arrested a half-dozen times (the official language of the charges was always interesting: "sauntering and loitering," "disorderly conduct," "failure to quit"). And traveling to Japan, and to North Vietnam, and speaking at hundreds of meetings and rallies, and helping a Catholic priest stay underground in defiance of the law.

I would have to recapture the scenes in a dozen courtrooms where I testified in the 1970s and 1980s. I would have to tell about the prisoners I have known, short-timers and lifers, and how they affected my view of imprisonment.

When I became a teacher I could not possibly keep out of the classroom my own experiences. I have often wondered how so many teachers manage to spend a year with a group of students and never reveal who they are, what kind of lives they have led, where their ideas come from, what they believe in, or what they want for themselves, for their students, and for the world.

Does not the very fact of that concealment teach something terrible—that you can separate the study of literature, history, philosophy, politics, the arts, from your own life, your deepest convictions about right and wrong?

In my teaching I never concealed my political views: my detestation of war and militarism, my anger at racial inequality, my belief in a democratic socialism, in a rational and just distribution of the world's wealth. I made clear my abhorrence of any kind of *bullying*, whether by powerful nations over weaker ones, governments over their citizens, employers over employees, or by anyone, on the Right or the Left, who thinks they have a monopoly on the truth.

This mixing of activism and teaching, this insistence that education cannot be neutral on the crucial issues of our time, this movement back and forth from the classroom to the struggles outside by teachers who hope their students will do the same, has always frightened the guardians of traditional education. They prefer that education simply prepare the new generation to take its proper place in the old order, not to question that order.

I would always begin a course by making it clear to my students that they would be getting *my* point of view, but that I would try to be fair to other points of view. I encouraged my students to disagree with me.

I didn't pretend to an objectivity that was neither possible nor desirable. "You can't be neutral on a moving train," I would tell them. Some were baffled by the metaphor, especially if they took it literally and tried to dissect its meaning. Others immediately saw what I meant: that events are already moving in certain deadly directions, and to be neutral means to accept that.

I never believed that I was imposing my views on blank slates, on innocent minds. My students had had a long period of political indoctrination before they arrived in my class—in the family, in high school, in the mass media. Into a marketplace so long dominated by orthodoxy I wanted only to wheel my little pushcart, offering my wares along with the others, leaving students to make their own choices.

The thousands of young people in my classes over the years gave me hope for the future. Through the seventies and the eighties, everyone outside seemed to be groaning about how "ignorant" and "passive" was the current generation of students. But listening to them, reading their journals and papers, and their reports on the community activity that was part of their assigned work, I was impressed with their sensitivity to injustice, their eagerness to be part of some good cause, their potential to change the world.

The student activism of the eighties was small in scale, but at that time there was no great national movement to join, and there were heavy economic pressures from all sides to "make good," to "be successful," to join the world of prosperous professionals. Still, many young people were yearning for something more, and so I did not despair. I remembered how in the fifties haughty observers talked of the "silent generation" as an immovable fact, and then, exploding that notion, came the sixties.

There's something else, more difficult to talk about, that has been crucial to my mood—my private life. How lucky I have been to live my life with a remarkable woman whose beauty, body and soul, I see again in our children and grandchildren. Roz shared and helped, worked as a social worker and a teacher, later made more of her talents as painter and musician. She loves literature and became first editor of everything I wrote. Living with her has given me a heightened sense of what is possible in this world.

And yet I am not oblivious to the bad news we are constantly confronted with. It surrounds me, inundates me, depresses me intermittently, angers me.

I think of the poor today, so many of them in the ghettos of the nonwhite, often living a few blocks away from fabulous wealth. I think of the hypocrisy of political leaders, of the control of information through deception, through omission. And of how, all over the world, governments play on national and ethnic hatred.

I am aware of the violence of everyday life for most of the human race. All represented by the images of children. Children hungry. Children with missing limbs. The bombing of children officially reported as "collateral damage."

As I write this, in the summer of 1993, there is a general mood of despair. The end of the cold war between the United States and the Soviet Union has not resulted in world peace. In the countries of the Soviet bloc there is desperation and disarray. There is a brutal war going on in the former Yugoslavia and more violence in Africa. The prosperous elite of the world finds it convenient to ignore starvation and sickness in poverty-ridden countries. The United States and other powers continue to sell arms wherever it is profitable, whatever the human costs.

In this country, the euphoria that accompanied the election in 1992 of a young and presumably progressive president has evaporated. The new political leadership of the country, like the old, seems to lack the vision, the boldness, the *will*, to break from the past. It maintains a huge military budget which distorts the economy and makes possible no more than puny efforts to redress the huge gap between rich and poor. Without such redress, the cities must remain riddled with violence and despair.

And there is no sign of a national movement to change this.

Only the corrective of historical perspective can lighten our gloom. Note how often in this century we have been *surprised*. By the sudden emergence of a people's movement, the sudden overthrow of a tyranny, the sudden coming to life of a flame we thought extinguished. We are surprised because we have not taken notice of the quiet simmerings of indignation, of the first faint sounds of protest, of the scattered signs of resistance that, in the midst of our despair, portend the excitement of change. The isolated acts begin to join, the individual thrusts blend into organized actions, and one day, often when the situation seems most hopeless, there bursts onto the scene a movement.

We are surprised because we don't see that beneath the surface of the present there is always the human material for change: the suppressed indignation, the common sense, the need for community, the love of children, the patience to wait for the right moment to act in concert with others. These are the elements that spring to the surface when a movement appears in history.

People are practical. They want change but feel powerless, alone, do not want to be the blade of grass that sticks up above the others and is cut down. They wait for a sign from someone else who will make the first move, or the second. And at certain times in history, there are intrepid people who take the risk that if they make that first move others will follow quickly enough to prevent their being cut down. And if we understand this, *we* might make that first move.

This is not a fantasy. This is how change has occurred again and again in the past, even the very recent past. We are so overwhelmed by the *present*, the flood of pictures and stories pouring in on us every day, drowning out this history, that it is no wonder if we lose hope.

I realize it is easier for me to feel hopeful because in many ways I have just been lucky.

Lucky, for one thing, to have escaped the circumstances of my childhood. There are memories of my father and mother, who met as immigrant factory workers, who worked hard all their lives and never got out of poverty. (I always feel some rage when I hear the voice of the arrogant and affluent: We have a wonderful system; if you work hard you will make it. How hard my parents worked.

How brave they were just to keep four sons alive in the cold-water tenements of Brooklyn.)

Lucky, after stumbling around from one bad job to another, to find work that I loved. Lucky to encounter remarkable people everywhere, to have so many good friends.

And also, lucky to be alive, because my two closest Air Force friends—Joe Perry, nineteen, and Ed Plotkin, twenty-six—died in the last weeks of the war. They were my buddies in basic training at Jefferson Barracks, Missouri. We marched in the summer heat together. We went out on weekend passes together. We learned to fly Piper Cubs in Vermont and played basketball in Santa Ana, California, while waiting for our assignments. Then Joe went to Italy as a bombardier, Ed to the Pacific as a navigator, I to England as a bombardier. Joe and I could write to one another, and I kidded him as we who flew B-17s kidded those who flew B-24s—we called them B-Dash-Two-Crash-Fours.

The night the European war ended, my crew drove to Norwich, the main city in East Anglia, where everybody was in the streets, wild with joy, the city ablaze with lights that had been out for six years. The beer flowed, enormous quantities of fish and chips were wrapped in newspapers and handed out to everyone, people danced and shouted and hugged one another.

A few days after that, my most recent letter to Joe Perry came back to me with a penciled notation on the envelope: "Deceased"— too quick a dismissal of a friend's life.

My crew flew our old battle-scarred B-17 back across the Atlantic, ready to continue bombing in the Pacific. Then came the news about the atomic bomb dropped on Hiroshima, and we were grateful—the war was over. (I had no idea that one day I would visit Hiroshima and meet blinded, maimed people who had survived the bomb, and that I would rethink that bombing and all the others.)

When the war ended and I was back in New York, I looked up Ed Plotkin's wife—he had stolen out of Fort Dix the night before he was being shipped overseas, to spend a last night with her. She told me Ed crashed in the Pacific and died just before the war ended and that a child was conceived the night he went AWOL. Years later, when I was teaching in Boston, someone came up to me after a class with a note: "Ed Plotkin's daughter wants to meet you." We met and I told her whatever I could remember about the father she never saw.

So I feel I have been given a gift—undeserved, just luck—of almost fifty years of life. I am always aware of that. For years after the war I had a recurrent dream. Two men would be walking in front of me in the street. They would turn, and it would be Joe and Ed.

Deep in my psyche, I think, is the idea that because I was so lucky and they were not, I owe them something. Sure, I want to have some fun; I have no desire to be a martyr, though I know some and admire them. Still, I owe it to Joe and Ed not to waste my gift, to use these years well, not just for myself but for that new world we all thought was promised by the war that took their lives.

And so I have no *right* to despair. I insist on hope.

It is a feeling, yes. But it is not irrational. People respect feelings but still want reasons. Reasons for going on, for not surrendering, for not retreating into private luxury or private desperation. People want evidence of those possibilities in human behavior I have talked about. I have suggested that there *are* reasons. I believe there *is* evidence. But too much to give to the questioner that night in Kalamazoo. It would take a book.

So I decided to write one.

PART ONE

The South and the Movement

Going South:
Spelman College

Teaching and living for seven years in the black community of
Spelman College in Atlanta, Georgia, in the years of "the Movement," I came to see the importance of small-scale actions as preparing the way for larger ones.

I did not seek out a "Negro college," in the year 1956, because
of an urge to do good. I was just looking for a job.

I had worked for three years loading trucks in a warehouse on
the four-to-midnight shift, while going to New York University
and Columbia. (I never paid a cent in tuition, thanks to the G.I. Bill
of Rights, still a good example of how governments can run vast
programs with minimum bureaucracy to enormous human bene-
fit.) One day I hurt my back lifting one eighty-pound carton too
many, and began to teach "part-time," learning quickly that part-
time teachers often work longer and get paid less than full-timers. I
taught four day courses at Upsala College, a Swedish-Lutheran, absurdly uptight college in New Jersey, and two evening courses at
absurdly chaotic Brooklyn College. So, from the "project" where
we lived in lower Manhattan I traveled an hour west to New Jersey

on some days, an hour east to Brooklyn other days, teaching six courses for a total of $3,000 a year.

Roz was doing secretarial work to help support us all. In high school, though editor of the literary magazine and winner of the English medal, she had taken typing and shorthand, as even the brightest of girls were expected to do. (Only when our children were grown up did she have a chance to go to college, teach English to "special students," that is, tough kids who were failing their courses, and then become a social worker, first with black high-school dropouts, afterwards with elderly poor people in the Italian-Irish sections of Boston. She wanted to give back, as she put it, what life had given her.)

Our children were in a nursery school for low-income families sponsored by good-hearted women of means who visited the school from time to time—they were all very tall and looked like Eleanor Roosevelt. Twice we went through the trauma of leaving a two-year-old crying inconsolably on the first day of nursery school, as we went off to our different destinations. One afternoon when I returned to pick up our son Jeff, he spotted me approaching, ran full speed to the schoolyard gate, and stuck his head between two of the bars; it took ten minutes to extricate him, with the help of a fireman and a crowbar.

Close to finishing my Ph.D. work in history at Columbia University, I was contacted by its placement bureau for an interview with the president of Spelman College, who was visiting New York. The idea of a "Negro college" hadn't occurred to me. Spelman at that time was virtually unknown to anyone outside the black community. He offered me the chairmanship of his history and social sciences department, and $4,000 a year. I summoned up my courage. "I have a wife and two kids. Could you make it $4,500?"

True, it was a tiny department, and scoffers might say being its chairman was like being the headwaiter in a two-waiter restaurant. But in my situation it was very welcome. I would still be poor, but prestigious.

While I had not sought out a teaching job in a black setting, my encounters with black people up to that time had made me open to the idea. My teenage reading (Upton Sinclair's *The Jungle*, John Steinbeck's *The Grapes of Wrath*, Richard Wright's *Native Son*) left me seeing race and class oppression as intertwined. Working in the Navy Yard I was conscious that black men were kept out of the craft unions for skilled workers, were given the toughest jobs on the ship as chippers and riveters, wielding dangerous steel tools driven by compressed air. In the Air Force I became painfully aware of the segregation of black soldiers in a war presumed to be against Hitler's racism. In our low-income housing project our friends and neighbors were Irish, Italians, African Americans, and Puerto Ricans, who worked together in a tenants' council and gathered for potluck dinners and basement dances.

In August of 1956, Roz and I trundled the two kids and our belongings into our ten-year-old Chevy and drove south. We arrived in Atlanta on a hot and rainy night, and Roz and the children (Myla was nine, Jeff almost seven) awoke to watch the shimmering wet lights on Ponce de Leon Avenue. We were in a different world, a thousand miles from home, a universe removed from the sidewalks of New York. Here was a city thick with foliage, fragrant with magnolias and honeysuckle. The air was sweeter and heavier. The people were blacker and whiter; through the raindrops on the windows they appeared as ghosts gliding through the darkness.

The campus of Spelman College was not far from the center of town, an oval garden of dogwood and magnolia trees, ringed with red-brick buildings. Our family was given temporary quarters in one of those buildings until we could find a place to live in town. That wasn't easy. Landlords wanted to know where I worked. When I told them I was teaching at Spelman, the atmosphere changed; apartments were no longer available. This was our first direct encounter with that malignancy which has for so long infected all of America but was then so much more visible in the Southern states.

What for us was an inconvenience was for blacks a daily and never-ending humiliation, and behind that a threat of violence to the point of murder. Just ten years earlier, a sheriff in Baker County, Georgia, taking a black man to jail, had smashed his head repeatedly with a blackjack, in view of witnesses. The man died. The sheriff, Claude Screws, was acquitted by a local jury, then found guilty by a federal jury under an old civil rights statute and sentenced to six months in prison. This was overturned by the Supreme Court, which found no proof that the sheriff had *intended* to deprive the prisoner of his constitutional rights. One day I looked down the list of members of the Georgia legislature and saw the name of Claude Screws.

The city of Atlanta at that time was as rigidly segregated as Johannesburg, South Africa. Peachtree Street, downtown, was white. Auburn Avenue ("sweet Auburn," as it was known in the Negro community) was a five-minute ride away from downtown, and was black. If black people were downtown it was because they were working for whites, or shopping at Rich's Department Store, where both races could come to buy but the cafeteria was for whites only. If a white person and a black person walked down the street together as equals, with no clear indication that the black was a servant of some kind, the atmosphere on the street suddenly became tense, threatening.

I began my classes. There were no white students at Spelman. My students, in a rich variety of colors, had wonderful names like Geneva, Herschelle, Marnesba, Aramintha. They were from all over the country, but most were from the South and had never had a white teacher. They were curious and shy, but the shyness disappeared after we came to know one another. Some were the daughters of the black middle class—of teachers, ministers, social workers, small business people, skilled workers. Others were the daughters of maids, porters, laborers, tenant farmers.

A college education for these young women was a matter of life and death. One of my students told me one day, sitting in my office, "My mother says I've got to do well, because I've already got two strikes against me. I'm black and I'm a woman. One more strike and I'm out."

And so they accepted—or seemed to accept—the tightly controlled atmosphere of Spelman College, where they were expected to dress a certain way, walk a certain way, pour tea a certain way.

There was compulsory chapel six times a week. Students had to sign in and out of their dormitories, and be in by 10:00 P.M. Their contacts with men were carefully monitored; the college authorities were determined to counter stories of the sexually free black woman and worse, the pregnant, unmarried black girl. Freshmen were not permitted to go across the street to the library at Atlanta University, where they might encounter the young men of Morehouse College. Trips into the city of Atlanta were closely supervised.

It was as if there was an unwritten, unspoken agreement between the white power structure of Atlanta and the administrations of the black colleges: We white folk will let you colored folk have your nice little college. You can educate your colored girls to service the Negro community, to become teachers and social workers, maybe even doctors or lawyers. We won't bother you. You can even have a few white faculty. At Christmas some of our white citizens may come to the Spelman campus to hear the famous Spelman choir. And in return, you will not interfere with our way of life.

This pact was symbolized by a twelve-foot-high stone wall around the campus, at certain points replaced by a barbed wire fence. After our family moved into an apartment on campus near that fence, our eight-year-old son, Jeff, who seemed to be an expert on such matters (at that time spending his spare hours with the buildings-and-grounds workers on campus), pointed out to us that the barbed wire was slanted not so as to keep intruders out, but to keep the Spelman students in.

One day the students would leap over that wall, climb over that barbed wire fence, but in the fall of 1956 there was no indication of that defiance. One year before, the bus boycott in Montgomery, Alabama, had ended in victory. The year before that, the Supreme Court had finally come around to deciding that the Fourteenth Amendment prohibited racial segregation in the public schools. Very little was done, however, to enforce that decision; the Supreme Court order stipulated "all deliberate speed," and the key word was not "speed."

I soon learned that beneath my students' politeness and decorum there was a lifetime of suppressed indignation. Once I asked them to write down their first memory of race prejudice, and the feelings tumbled out.

One told how as a teenager she sat down in the front of a bus next to a white woman. "This woman immediately stormed out of her seat, trampling over my legs and feet, and cursing under her breath. Other white passengers began to curse under their breaths. Never had I seen people staring at me as if they hated me. Never had I really experienced being directly rejected as though I were some poisonous, venomous creature."

A student from Forsyth, Georgia, wrote: "I guess if you are from a small Georgia town, as I am, you can say that your first encounter with prejudice was the day you were born. . . . My parents never got to see their infant twins alive because the only incubator in the hospital was on the 'white' side."

Every one, without exception, had some similar early experience. Years before I came to Atlanta I had read Countee Cullen's poem "Incident":

> Once riding in Old Baltimore,
> Heart-filled, head-filled with glee,
> I saw a Baltimorean
> Keep looking straight at me.
>
> Now I was eight and very small,
> And he was no whit bigger,
> And so I smiled, but he poked out
> His tongue, and called me, "Nigger."
>
> I saw the whole of Baltimore
> From May until December;
> Of all the things that happened there
> That's all that I remember.

That poem, which I read when I was perhaps nineteen, affected me powerfully. What I had known in my head about race prejudice now touched my heart; I was, for a moment, that eight-year-old boy. Perhaps we respond so quickly to injustice against children because we remember the helpless innocence of our own childhood, when we are all especially vulnerable to humiliation. My students' stories of their own early experiences affected me the same way.

The events of my life, growing up poor, working in a shipyard, being in a war, had nurtured an indignation against the bullies of the world, those who used wealth or military might or social status to keep others down. And now I was in the midst of a situation where human beings, by accident of birth, because of their skin color, were being treated as inferior beings. I knew that it was wrong for me, a white teacher, to lead the way. But I was open to anything my students wanted to do, refusing to accept the idea that a teacher should confine his teaching to the classroom when so much was at stake outside it.

I had been at Spelman six months when, in January of 1957, my students and I had a small encounter with the Georgia state legislature. We had decided to visit one of its sessions. Our intent was simply to watch the legislature go about its business. But when we arrived we saw, and should have expected, that the gallery had a small section on the side marked "colored." The students conferred and quickly decided to ignore the signs and sit in the main section, which was quite empty. Listening to the legislators drone on, even for a few minutes, about a bill on fishing rights in Georgia rivers, we could understand why the gallery was empty.

As our group of about thirty filed into the seats, panic broke out. The fishing bill was forgotten. The Speaker of the House seemed to be having an apoplectic fit. He rushed to the microphone and shouted, "You nigras get over to where you belong! We got segregation in the state of Georgia."

The members of the legislature were now standing in their seats and shouting up at us, the sounds echoing strangely in the huge domed chamber. The regular business was forgotten. Police appeared quickly and moved threateningly towards our group.

We conferred again while the tension in the chamber thickened. Students were not yet ready, in those years before the South rose up en masse, to be arrested. We decided to move out into the hall and then come back into the "colored" section, me included.

What followed was one of those strange scenes that the paradoxes of the racist, courteous South often produced. A guard came up to me, staring very closely, apparently not able to decide if I was "white" or "colored," then asked where this group of visitors was from. I told him. A moment later, the Speaker of the House went up to the microphone, again interrupting a legislator, and intoned, "The members of the Georgia state legislature would like to extend a warm welcome to the visiting delegation from Spelman College."

A few male students from Morehouse College were with us on that trip. One of them was Julian Bond, son of the distinguished educator and former president of Lincoln University, Horace Mann Bond. Julian was an occasional visitor at our house on the Spelman campus, introducing us to the records of Ray Charles, bringing poems he had written. (A decade later, Julian, by then a well-known civil rights leader, would be elected to the Georgia state legislature and, in an odd reprise of our experience, would be expelled by his fellow legislators because of his outspoken opposition to the war in Vietnam. A Supreme Court decision upholding his right to free speech restored him to his seat.)

Sometime in early 1959, I suggested to the Spelman Social Science Club, to which I was faculty adviser, that it might be interesting to undertake some real project involving social change. The discussion became very lively. Someone said, "Why don't we try to do something about the segregation of the public libraries?" And so, two years before sit-ins swept the South and "the Movement" excited the nation, a few young women at Spelman College decided to launch an attack on the racial policy of the main library in Atlanta.

It was a nonviolent assault. Black students would enter the Carnegie Library, to the stares of everyone around, and ask for John Locke's *An Essay Concerning Human Understanding*, or John Stuart Mill's *On Liberty*, or Tom Paine's *Common Sense*. Turned away with evasive answers ("We'll send a copy to your Negro branch"), they kept coming back, asking for the Declaration of Independence, the Constitution of the United States, and other choices designed to make sensitive librarians uneasy.

The pressure on the libraries was stepped up. We let it be known that a lawsuit was next. One of the plaintiffs would be a professor of French at Spelman, Dr. Irene Dobbs Jackson, who came from a prominent Atlanta family. Her sister was Mattiwilda Dobbs, the distinguished opera singer. Her father was John Wesley Dobbs, a great orator in the old Southern tradition. (Once, sitting in the Wheat Street Baptist Church, I heard John Wesley Dobbs keep a crowd of a thousand in an uproar. "My Mattiwilda was asked to sing here in Atlanta," he thundered. "But she said, 'No sir. Not while my daddy has to sit in the balcony!'" Years later, Irene Jackson's son, Maynard Jackson, would be elected mayor of Atlanta. That was impossible to imagine in those days when we were pressing for something so absurdly simple as the right of black people to go to the library.)

In the midst of our campaign, I was sitting in the office of Whitney Young, Dean of the School of Social Work of Atlanta University, who was working with us. We were talking about what our next moves should be when the phone rang. It was a member of the Library Board. Whitney listened, said, "Thank you," and hung up. He smiled. The board had decided to end the policy of racial segregation in the Atlanta library system.

A few days after that, four of us rode downtown to the Carnegie Library: Dr. Irene Jackson; Earl Sanders, a young black professor of music at Spelman; Pat West, the white Alabama-born wife of Henry West, who taught philosophy in my department at Spelman; and myself. As the youngish librarian handed a new library membership card to Irene Jackson, she spoke calmly but her hand trembled slightly. She understood that a bit of history was being made.

Pat and Henry West, white Southerners who had scandalized their families by coming to live in a black community, had a three-year-old boy who was the first and only white child in the Spelman College nursery school. At Christmastime it was traditional for schoolchildren to be taken to meet Santa Claus at Rich's Department Store downtown, where the children would take turns sitting on Santa's lap and whispering what they wanted for Christmas. Santa was a white man in need of a job, and he had no qualms about holding little black kids on his lap. When little Henry West climbed onto his lap, Santa Claus stared at him, looked at the other children, then back at Henry, and whispered in his ear, "Boy, you white or colored?" The nursery school teacher stood by, listening. Henry answered, "I want a bicycle."

I have told about the modest campaign to desegregate Atlanta's libraries because the history of social movements often confines itself to the large events, the pivotal moments. Typically, surveys of the history of the civil rights movement deal with the Supreme Court decision in the Brown case, the Montgomery bus boycott, the sit-ins, the Freedom Rides, the Birmingham demonstrations, the March on Washington, the Civil Rights Act of 1964, the march from Selma to Montgomery, the Voting Rights Act of 1965.

Missing from such histories are the countless small actions of unknown people that led up to those great moments. When we understand this, we can see that the tiniest acts of protest in which we engage may become the invisible roots of social change.

Sitting in our living room on the Spelman campus one evening, Dr. Otis Smith, a physician, told of his recent departure from Fort Valley, Georgia, an agricultural town of twelve thousand people where he had been the only black doctor. "Run out of town." He smiled. "It sounds like something out of an old Western movie."

Dr. Smith had been a star athlete for Morehouse College, and then a student at Meharry Medical School in Nashville; he'd accepted an offer from Georgia's Board of Regents to help pay for his last year in medical school in return for a promise to spend fifteen months in a rural area in Georgia. Fort Valley, in Peach County, seemed a likely place. The last black doctor in town had died several years before, leaving blacks there (60 percent of the population) at the mercy of those humiliations that often accompanied white doctor–colored patient relations in the Deep South: entrance through the side door, a special "colored" waiting room, and sometimes the question, Do you have the money? before a sick call was made to the house.

Otis Smith made a down payment on a home, hung out his shingle, and soon his office was full. But when he showed up at the Fort Valley Hospital for his first obstetrical stint in the town, the two white nurses stared at him and left the room, with a black woman in labor on the table. He delivered the baby with the aid of a black attendant.

One evening, while he was talking on the telephone to a patient who needed his help, a white woman cut in on the party line and demanded that he get off so she could speak. He told her he was a doctor talking to a patient. She replied, "Get off the phone, nigger." Perhaps an old-style Negro doctor would have responded differently, but the young Dr. Smith said, "Get off the phone yourself, you bitch."

He was arrested the next day, brought into court before his attorney even knew that the trial was going to take place, and sentenced to eight months on the chain gang for using obscene language to a white woman. In prison, facing the chain gang, he was offered release if he would leave town immediately. The next day the black people of Fort Valley were without their doctor.

In Georgia, as all over the South, in the "quiet" years before the eruption of the sit-ins there were individual acts—obscure, unrecorded, sometimes seemingly futile—which kept the spirit of defiance alive. They were often bitter experiences, but they nurtured the anger that would one day become a great force and change the South forever.

"Young Ladies
Who Can Picket"

On the surface, the South in the 1950s seemed at peace. But in the five years between the Montgomery boycott and the historic sit-ins of 1960 there were sit-ins in sixteen cities. Like so many acts of resistance that take place all the time in this large country, they did not get national attention; the media, like the politicians, do not take note of rebellion until it is too large to be ignored.

At Spelman College, at Morehouse College, at the other four Negro colleges of the Atlanta University system in those years, all appeared to be quiet, and looking at the surface of things, it seemed as if it would always be that way. One of the important things I learned at Spelman is that it's easy to mistake silence for acceptance.

At the beginning of February 1960, on radio, on television, in the press, the news came that four black college students in Greensboro, North Carolina, had occupied stools at a Woolworth lunch counter and refused to move, and that similar "sit-ins" were spreading quickly to other cities in North Carolina, Virginia, Tennessee—then Florida, South Carolina, Alabama, and Texas.

In Atlanta, Julian Bond and another Morehouse student, football star Lonnie King, went into action. They contacted students from the other black colleges connected with Atlanta University—Spelman, Clark, Morris Brown, the Theological Center—and began making plans.

The college presidents, hearing of this, took steps to cool the militancy of the students. They wanted to avoid sit-ins, demonstrations, picket lines. They suggested instead that the students take out a full-page advertisement in the *Atlanta Constitution* outlining their grievances. To encourage this, the presidents promised they would raise the money for the ad.

The students accepted the offer but secretly decided that the ad would be used as a springboard for direct action. The Spelman student president, Roslyn Pope, a student of mine who had become a friend of the family, came to the house one day asking to use our typewriter.

The year before, just after her return from a scholarship year in Paris, she and I had been arrested together as I drove her off-campus one evening to her parents' home in Atlanta. Flooding my car with their searchlight, two policemen ordered us into their patrol car.

"Why are you arresting us?" I asked. (Roslyn was silent. I imagined her measuring the moral distance between Atlanta and Paris.)

"Disorderly conduct."

"What's disorderly about our conduct?"

Smacking his flashlight into his palm, he said, "You sitting in a car with a nigger gal and asking me what's disorderly conduct?"

We spent much of the night in jail, in separate lockups—each a large communal cell harboring a bunch of hard-luck characters of all ages and conditions. (Jails were doubly segregated, by sex and by race.) When I asked to make a phone call—the arrested person's sacred right, in the mythology of American justice—the guard pointed to a dilapidated pay phone in the corner. I had no change, but a fellow prisoner offered a dime. The coin dropped. The phone was dead. I looked down—the wires had been severed. I held the two ends together with one hand, dialed with the other, and managed to reach Don Hollowell, a young black lawyer whose bold demeanor in court I had admired. He came in the early hours of the morning and got us out. The charges were later dropped.

Visiting us now, a year later, Roslyn Pope was working on the first draft of the statement planned by the student leaders. She was an English major, a fine writer, and we could see immediately that it would be an extraordinary document.

It appeared March 9, 1960, dramatically, on a full page of the *Constitution* under a huge headline, "AN APPEAL FOR HUMAN RIGHTS," and it created a sensation:

> We . . . have joined our hearts, minds, and bodies in the cause of gaining those rights which are inherently ours as members of the human race and as citizens of the United States. . . .
>
> We do not intend to wait placidly for those rights which are already legally and morally ours to be meted out to us one at a time. . . . We want to state clearly and unequivocally that we cannot tolerate, in a nation professing democracy and among people professing Christianity, the discriminatory conditions under which the Negro is living today in Atlanta, Georgia.

The appeal went on to catalogue very specifically the wrongs committed against black people by the system of segregation in education, jobs, housing, voting, hospitals, concerts, movies, restaurants, law enforcement. It concluded with words that for the students were a code forecasting their plan of action: "We must say in all candor that we plan to use every legal and nonviolent means at our disposal to secure full citizenship rights as members of this great democracy of ours."

The governor of Georgia, Ernest Vandiver, was furious. The appeal was "an anti-American document . . . obviously not written by students." Furthermore, the governor said, "it does not sound like it was written in this country."

Five days later, my wife and I were at a student party when I was drawn aside and told of the plan: at eleven o'clock the next morning, hundreds of students would sit in at ten cafeterias in downtown Atlanta. They wanted me to telephone the press just a few minutes before eleven, so as not to tip off the police.

The next morning, at about ten o'clock, six Spelman students came to our house on campus to borrow our car. They needed it, they said, smiling, "to go downtown." I waited until exactly eleven o'clock to make the call. I could hear the editor on the other end of the telephone calling out assignments to reporters as I gave him the names of the cafeterias.

It was a beautifully organized action. Several hundred students had gone downtown, in small groups, to different cafeterias, and at the stroke of eleven, they took seats and refused to move. Seventy-seven were arrested, including fourteen students from Spelman. Of those fourteen, thirteen were from the Deep South—places like Bennettsville, South Carolina, Bainbridge, Georgia, and Ocala, Florida—the Faulknerian small towns of traditional Negro submissiveness.

Among the "Spelman girls" arrested was another of my students, Marian Wright. A photo that appeared all over the country shows Marian sitting quietly behind bars, reading C. S. Lewis's book *The Screwtape Letters*.

The students were released on bail, charged with multiple counts of conspiracy, breaching the peace, intimidating restaurant owners, and refusing to leave the premises. The possible prison sentences for each added up to ninety years. But the rush of events in Atlanta and the South soon overwhelmed the system, and their cases were never brought to trial.

It was the beginning of an assault on racial segregation in Atlanta—and also on the long tradition of gentility, silence, and abstinence from social struggle which had marked Spelman College during its seventy-five years of existence. The "Spelman girls" would not be the same. Demonstrations, boycotts, and picketing would become part of the life of these black young women. And this would cause tremors among the conservative administrators and trustees of the college.

Some of the faculty were also unhappy. A black professor of political science wrote a letter to the *Atlanta Constitution* deploring the students' actions, saying they were missing their classes and hurting their education. To me, they were furthering their education in a way that could not be matched by a dozen courses in political science.

Marian Wright, in the midst of all that followed the sit-ins, walked into our apartment on campus one day carrying a notice she was about to post in her dormitory. Its heading combined perfectly the past and the present of the "Spelman girl." It read, "Young Ladies Who Can Picket, Please Sign Below."

(Marian would go on to Yale Law School. She would become the first black woman lawyer in Mississippi, marry civil rights lawyer Peter Edelman, start the Children's Defense Fund in Washington, D.C., and become a powerful, eloquent voice throughout the nation, declaring for the rights of children and mothers as against the demands of a war economy. Our friendship has continued through those years.)

Our family life in Atlanta was not "normal." It seemed that there were always meetings of some sort in our apartment on campus, while the kids tried to do homework in their rooms. With the Atlanta school system still segregated, Myla and Jeff were going to all-white schools not far from Spelman.

Roz and I knew that the complications of race in a time of turmoil were a heavy burden for children to bear, and we were proud of how stalwart ours were, Jeff bringing his white school chums back to campus to play with the neighborhood black kids, Myla befriending the first black girl to be admitted to her high school.

We tried our best not to make them feel that they had to be political heroes. But there was no way they could not *feel* the pressure to "do right" in those tense years in the South, when moral dilemmas presented themselves every day. We made sure not to say anything when they kept their cool distance from the things going on around them, perhaps in defiance of their parents' intense involvement. But it was good to be surprised every once in a while. In the fall of 1962, during the Cuban missile crisis, with nuclear threat in the air, we were on a picket line in downtown Atlanta, calling for a peaceful solution. Myla was fifteen. Like her mother, she was involved in local theater at that time, and had been cast for the title role in *The Diary of Anne Frank*. She had been featured in the newspaper publicity surrounding the coming production, and we expected that she would not want to complicate her situation by getting involved in controversial politics.

But that day she suddenly appeared on the picket line. The reporters on the scene crowded around her to get some comment. She simply said her presence spoke for itself.

Roz had immediate rapport with the students and faculty in the black colleges. The Atlanta-Morehouse-Spelman Players, a superbly talented company, enlisted her to join the cast of the musical *The King and I*, to play the role of the white British teacher of the King's children.

The role of the King of Siam was played by a tall, powerfully built, very black young man, a Morehouse football player named Johnny Popwell. With his head shaved he looked properly fierce. On opening night, in the famous dance-lesson sequence when the King says, "No, this is not the way Europeans dance," and Johnny Popwell put his arm firmly around Roz's waist to dance with her, there was an audible murmur in the audience. In the year 1959 that was a bold theatrical event.

Living in Atlanta those seven tumultuous years, I learned not to trust the Northern stereotype of white Southerners as incorrigible racists. Yankee self-righteousness ignored the depth of race hatred in places like Boston or New York. And everyone is capable of change as circumstances change. The change might only be in response to self-interest, but that is a beginning, leading to deeper changes in thought and behavior.

The self-interest that motivates behavioral change is often based on the simple but inexorable pull of financial gain. For instance, in 1959 the Georgia General Assembly overwhelmingly approved a resolution calling for the impeachment of six justices of the U.S. Supreme Court for overly liberal decisions. Shortly afterward, it refused to pass a resolution banning interracial sports in Georgia. The impeachment resolution cost nothing; the banning of interracial sports would have made it impossible for the Georgia baseball team to remain in the South Atlantic League, and thus would have lost much revenue for the state. Similarly, Atlanta firemen said they would not work if the fire department became racially mixed, but when blacks were hired they stayed on the job.

Another force working for change in race relations has been political power, as when racist politicians, seeking black votes, change their tune. The arch-segregationist Governor George Wallace of Alabama made a startling about-face after the Voting Rights Act became law. In Atlanta, as more blacks voted, Mayor William Hartsfield, a longtime segregationist, began to alter his viewpoint.

Change was evident in the spring of 1960, when the musical company of *My Fair Lady* came to play in the Atlanta Municipal Auditorium, which had a special section in the balcony for blacks. A half-dozen members of the Atlanta-Morehouse-Spelman troupe decided to attend, but were determined to sit in the main section of the orchestra. Henry West went downtown to buy a group of tickets for the first rows in the orchestra, the best seats in the house.

The actors, including the Othello-like director, J. Preston Cochrane, all elegantly dressed, presented their tickets and swept past the ticket-taker to their seats before he could recover from his surprise. The manager asked them to move; they showed the stubs of their tickets. He said the show would not go on unless they moved. They said they could wait. The other theatregoers were not making a fuss, they pointed out. Indeed, the whites occupying the seats near them had come to see a musical, not to fight the Civil War.

The manager, much upset, went back to his office and phoned Mayor Hartsfield at home to tell him what was happening. Hartsfield thought a moment, then drawled, "The only suggestion I can make is that you dim the lights." The show went on, and it was the beginning of the end of racial segregation at the Atlanta Municipal Auditorium.

As an atmosphere begins to change, people adapt, discarding long-held habits. A Spelman student told of riding an Atlanta bus the morning after a federal court ruled that the races could no longer be separated on public buses. She watched a black man get on the bus and sit down in a front seat. An indignant white woman demanded that the bus driver move the man. The driver turned. "Ma'am, don't you read the newspapers?" She insisted that he stop the bus and she hailed a policeman. The policeman boarded the bus, listened to her, and said, "Ma'am, don't you read the newspapers?"

There have always been Southern whites who, at great risk, pioneered in the movement for racial justice. I was lucky to know some of them: Myles Horton, founder of the Highlander Folk School in Tennessee; Carl and Anne Braden, editors of the *Southern Courier* in Louisville, Kentucky; Pat Watters and Margaret Long, journalists with the *Atlanta Constitution*; reporters Fred Powledge and Jack Nelson. As the black movement began shaking things up, many others, their sense of outrage long suppressed, were encouraged to take a stand.

What has been accomplished these last few decades by the struggles and sacrifices of people in the civil rights movement in changing the consciousness of both blacks and whites can only be called a beginning. Every day there are stories that show the persistence of racism in this country. But not to recognize or to underplay the movement's accomplishment is to discourage the new generation from participating in what will be a long, slow struggle, not *for* equality (that phrase suggests completion), but *toward* equality.

What took place in Atlanta was a combination of frontal assaults—sit-ins, demonstrations, arrests—and a persistent, stubborn wearing away of the encrusted rules of racial segregation. In that decade we heard the word "revolution" thrown about. To some people it meant armed rebellion. To me it came to mean just such a combination of daring forays and patient pushing-pushing-pushing as I saw in the South, "the long march through the institutions," as someone described it—not a completed event, but an ongoing process.

As I began to realize, no pitifully small picket line, no poorly attended meeting, no tossing out of an idea to an audience or even to an individual should be scorned as insignificant.

The power of a bold idea uttered publicly in defiance of dominant opinion cannot be easily measured. Those special people who speak out in such a way as to shake up not only the self-assurance of their enemies, but the complacency of their friends, are precious catalysts for change.

I remember driving to the Atlanta airport (much of my truly revolutionary history has consisted of driving to airports) to pick up E. Franklin Frazier, a black man and a world-famous sociologist, author of the classic *The Negro Family in America*. He had just arrived from France and was coming to speak in the Atlanta University Center.

He was a stocky man of medium height, wearing a jaunty beret. When they refused to serve us a cup of coffee at the airport cafeteria, he said, smiling to the waitress, "This is interesting. Last week I had coffee with the president of France, and this week I'm refused coffee in Atlanta."

Frazier's trip to Atlanta caused great excitement. He had been run out of the city as a young man when he published a blistering article on "The White Southerner." His Atlanta friends remembered him as an irascible, fearless person who refused to cater to white notions of how black people should behave. He smoked cigars, drank whiskey, and used direct, pungent language, as if in a calculated affront to those blacks who, in an effort to assimilate, cultivated the manners of the smart set and the vocabulary of pedants.

His most recent book at the time, *Black Bourgeoisie*, was a critical, sometimes excoriating look at affluent blacks in the United States and had aroused bitter controversy in the black community. Frazier said that the Negro middle class had borrowed its bourgeois style and traditional religion from the white middle class, which was itself intellectually and culturally barren. Black people should look to their own heritage, he said, create their own culture. I thought of Frazier years later when I listened to Malcolm X.

The lecture hall on the Spelman campus was jam-packed, with people sitting in the aisles, on window sills, in every square foot of space. Frazier was unsparing in his attack on American racism, but also on what he saw as subservience and conservatism among blacks. He denounced those black newspapers and magazines that created a world of "make-believe" in which successful businessmen were the heroes.

It was the job of education, he said, to smash through this make-believe and give black people a realistic picture of themselves and of the world. "Most of our schools are finishing schools for the Negro middle class," he told the audience that night. "I went to compulsory chapel in college for four years, and I heard nothing in those four years but sugary, sentimental slop!" He was not directing a special attack on his own people, he assured us. "We have never invented any crimes or sins that white people hadn't already perfected."

In the question period someone asked, "Why did you write so harshly in *Black Bourgeoisie*?" His response brought laughter and applause from the audience: "My friend, white people have bamboozled us. Preachers have bamboozled us. Teachers have bamboozled us, and kept us all bamboozled. We need someone to debamboozle us!"

I was struck by Frazier's willingness to hurl challenges one after the other, like a fearless David, at the Goliath of American racism, not checking first to see if anyone would join him. He had faith that if he spoke truth, however unpopular at first, others would gather around, and ideas first scorned would be more and more accepted. In the years to come, I was much encouraged by his example.

That June the student movement planned a small sit-in at the lunch counter of Rich's Department Store. There were no stools at the counter itself, but there were tables and chairs where people could sit after they bought their food. Roz and I took the assignment of going to the counter, each buying two cups of coffee and two sandwiches. We sat down at a table. Two black students, John Gibson and Carolyn Long, who had been browsing through records nearby, now sat down with us and we all began to have our meal. Another foursome was doing the same at the other end of the lunch area.

We were asked to leave but we didn't. The Rich's managers did not call the police, wanting to avoid public attention to a policy that was becoming more and more embarrassing; they just shut down the lunch counter, put out the lights, and began putting chairs up on tables all around us. A crowd of white shoppers gathered around, muttering angrily that we were preventing them from getting their lunch. More black students, including Lonnie King, joined us at our table. We sat there in the semidarkness, chatting, until the store was about to close, and then we left, our point made.

It took more sit-ins, more arrests, and a boycott of Rich's by its substantial black clientele, but in the fall of 1961 Rich's and a number of other restaurants in Atlanta agreed to end their policy of racial segregation. What had seemed fixed could change, what had seemed immovable could move.

"A President Is
Like a Gardener"

These administrators assume that we're savages and that it's their job to civilize us." This was the comment of one of my students at Spelman, an English major, on the lack of freedom at the college, the antiquated restrictions, the finishing-school atmosphere, the paternalism and control. And when "the Spelman girls" emerged from jail and returned to campus, they were in no mood to accept what they had accepted before.

Their rebellion came to a head in the spring of 1963, but it had been building up for years. Shortly after I arrived at the college, a star student named Herschelle Sullivan (later she received a doctorate from Columbia University and worked for the U.N. in Africa) wrote an editorial for the student newspaper, an allegory chiding the college for its tight control of students. One of the figures in the allegory was a lion guarding the gate, not allowing young people to explore the world beyond, and Herschelle used the phrase "benevolent despotism." She was called in by President Albert Manley and chastised for writing the editorial. He also criticized the editor of the newspaper for printing it.

Manley, a courtly, handsome man, was Spelman's first black president. His predecessors had been white New England women missionaries. He was cautious and conservative, obviously made uneasy by the new militant currents moving through black campuses. Also, he had to answer to the Board of Trustees, which included several Rockefellers and a number of white businesspeople from the North.

After the incident with Herschelle Sullivan, I felt she needed support and that I should not remain silent if one of my students, perhaps influenced by my classes, spoke her mind freely about what troubled her on campus. I wrote a long letter to Dr. Manley, saying that in my classes in American history and Western civilization I had been stressing the need for independent thought, for courage in the face of repression, and that any administrative effort to discourage freedom of expression was a blow at all of the values crucial to liberal arts education. I received no reply.

Five other faculty members wrote to President Manley expressing their concern that the intellectual and social growth of students at Spelman was limited by needless restrictions, and suggesting that students should be encouraged to develop self-discipline rather than have discipline thrust upon them. They too received no reply. But clearly a conflict was growing.

When the sit-in movement erupted in Atlanta in the spring of 1960, I wrote an article for *The Nation* about the participation of Spelman students and noted that the traditional Spelman emphasis on turning out "young ladies" was being challenged, that the new-type Spelman student was to be found on the picket line, or in jail. I learned that President Manley resented the article for its criticism of the college as it was.

In the spring of 1962, students were stimulated by the visit of Spelman alumna Marian Wright, then at Yale Law School, who spoke to them about young people becoming a force for social change. Shortly after her departure, a group of students addressed a petition to the Spelman administration. They respectfully acknowledged Spelman's "productive past," but said the college was "not preparing today's woman to assume the responsibilities of today's rapidly changing world. . . . The acquisition of knowledge is impaired by the conspicuous absence of an atmosphere conducive to intellectual curiosity and the pursuit of excellence." They asked for "first steps" to create a new atmosphere, a liberalizing of the rules, modernization of the curriculum, improvement of library facilities.

A meeting was called to publicize the petition and there was a huge turnout. More than three hundred young women, over half the student body, signed the petition. An honors student named Lana Taylor chaired the meeting.

President Manley responded angrily. He called in student leaders, including Lana Taylor, and berated them for circulating the petition, saying they should have utilized "regular channels." He said that if students didn't like the situation at Spelman they could leave. He demanded that the student newspaper, which was planning to include the petition in its forthcoming issue, not print it. The editor later said it was "like a decree. . . . I didn't feel I had any choice but to obey."

That summer of 1962, Lana Taylor received a letter from the college informing her that her request for a scholarship had been denied on the ground of "poor citizenship." (In May she had been elected president of the senior class.)

In the spring of 1963 matters came to a head. The Social Science Club decided to call a meeting to air some of the issues of campus life. I was the club's advisor, but I did not initiate the idea. The topic for the evening was "On Liberty at Spelman," and faculty, administration, and students were all invited. A dozen faculty came. Some administrators were there, but Dr. Manley said he had another engagement. The room, which usually held about thirty or forty students, was packed with over two hundred. The meeting was chaired by Dorcas Boit, a student from Kenya.

Student after student rose to denounce the administration for indignities they had experienced—surveillance, paternalism, authoritarianism—and to express their fears. "We are afraid that if we sign anything we won't graduate. You're afraid to say something. You're afraid somebody might call you in." Students told of not being allowed to leave their rooms because they did not attend a concert being given on campus.

Marie Thomas, who had won Spelman's award for artistic achievement and was one of five theater people suspended for a semester because they had attended a cast party "after hours" (she went on to a successful career on the New York stage), sent a letter to be read to the meeting. It spoke passionately against "our traditional, antiquated, medieval, and aged standards, rules and regulations. . . . What do they mean to a modern girl growing normally and learning in our modern world today? Times have indeed changed. God give us the strength, knowledge and understanding to change with them." The students greeted her letter with tremendous applause.

At a faculty meeting chaired by President Manley, I proposed that he and my colleagues listen to a tape of that student meeting to get a sense of their grievances. Manley refused. It was becoming clear that he saw me as an instigator rather than simply a supporter of the protests. When students begin to defy established authority it often appears to besieged administrators that "someone must be behind this," the implication being that young people are incapable of thinking or acting on their own.

After that faculty meeting I went to see Dr. Manley, hoping to ease the tension between us. Our house on campus was near the Manleys', we'd had dinner several times at their home, and our relations had been friendly if somewhat formal. The following is drawn from the journal I kept that first half of 1963:

> Conference with Manley. I had asked for it to try to generate some cordiality in face to face encounter after tension of last meeting. No cordiality, perhaps slight easing of tension, but absolutely no agreement on anything. On the Social Science Club meeting. "You should have cleared it with me first." I said that was intolerable— that on a democratic campus any group should be able to meet any time on any subject without clearing it with anyone. He said, as he kept saying throughout—"that's where we disagree". . . . He said, "Why do you keep bringing up these things? Why aren't you interested in other things, students cheating on exams, students stealing

in dormitories, things missing all the time? Aren't you interested in these things?" Not very much I said. Yes, I said, I'm interested in everything, but some things are more important. He said at one point: "I have never been a crusader and I am not now." At the end of the meeting I said, you put your finger on the heart of it when you said you aren't a crusader. Perhaps I am somewhat. But whatever we are, shouldn't we want to turn out students who have something of the crusader in them? No response.

I felt a certain sympathy for President Manley—he was under pressure from all sides, the Board of Trustees, other college presidents, perhaps important people in the black community—I didn't really know. But I was moved by the students, their courage in finally speaking their minds. One student, who had resisted an attempt by an administration person to censor a speech of hers, said, "Spelman is like a coffin. You have to fit it exactly either by stretching or shrinking. But nothing must stick out—not a toe, not a hand, not a hair." Another student, who left in her senior year, wrote back explaining her departure: "I just got tired of being agitated and locked up. . . . I like the girls at Spelman, but I will never have any real love of the place, because it offers me nothing to love. . . . To me, college is a place where the student grows. But how can one grow any way but warped when one lives under warped conditions?"

In late April there was a testimonial dinner in honor of Dr. Manley's tenth year at Spelman. I walked over to the dining hall with Charles Merrill, a Boston educator who sponsored scholarships abroad for outstanding Spelman students. He was perhaps the lone voice for liberalism on the Spelman Board of Trustees. We had been on friendly terms for years, and he joked, "Should I walk with you? . . . Will they put you at a table by yourself?" The main speaker at the dinner was the chairman of Spelman's trustees, Lawrence McGregor, a New Jersey banker, who gave a hint of what was coming (this is also from my journal): "A president is like a gardener—he must make sure things grow in their place—and if anything grows where it's not supposed to grow he must get rid of it."

Two months later, in June of 1963, with the semester over, students gone, and the campus empty, my family packed the old Chevy to go north for the summer. They got into the car, and I asked them to wait a moment while I went to the mailbox to pick up the mail.

There was a letter from the Office of the President. "The College does not intend to renew your employment at the end of your present term, and you are hereby notified of that fact. . . . Accordingly, you are relieved of all duties with the College after June 30, 1963, and you will be expected to vacate your apartment by June 30, 1963. The College's check for your termination pay is enclosed." There was a check for $7,000, one year's salary.

It was a shock. Despite the conflict, which had become intense, I had not expected this. It was clear now why everyone's letters of reappointment for the next year had been held up for two months, with various excuses given—Manley was waiting until all students were off the campus and this could be done without an uproar.

I walked back to the car, told Roz and the children that we had to talk before leaving. We reopened the apartment and sat down in the living room, where I read the letter to them. Roz was stunned. Myla and Jeff were indignant. Myla had been campaigning for years for us to move from Atlanta, but now she said, "We won't leave!"

Staughton Lynd, our campus neighbor and my departmental pal, seeing our car still there, walked in. Staughton and his wife, Alice, had just returned from visiting the hospital to see their little boy, who had been seriously injured in a fall.

I told Staughton that he had enough on his mind, should tend to his family. But he, indomitable as always, immediately got on the phone to spread the word and round up help. The reaction seemed to split along generational lines. Veteran faculty were hesitant to speak up. The younger black professors rushed to my support—Lois Moreland, in my department, an NAACP activist; Samuel DuBois Cook, political science professor at Atlanta University and a former Morehouse classmate of Martin Luther King, Jr.; Shirley McBay, a new and therefore especially vulnerable and especially brave young math teacher. (Later, Moreland would remain at Spelman; Cook would become a college president in New Orleans, McBay a dean of students at M.I.T.)

A few white colleagues from the English department joined the campaign to annul my dismissal—Renate Wolf, a German-born novelist, Esta Seaton, a poet. But President Manley was adamant. To visiting delegations he gave the reason he had not put in the letter. I was "insubordinate." (It was true, I suppose.)

I wanted to fight the dismissal and was sure I was on good legal ground. I was chair of the department, a full professor with tenure, and by all the rules of the profession I could not be summarily fired. When I called Don Hollowell for legal advice, he was confident that Manley had broken my contract with the college. And yes, he said, he would take the case. When I called the American Association of University Professors in Washington they were sure my tenure rights had been violated, and they would set up a committee to investigate.

But by this time I was acutely conscious of the gap between law and justice. I knew that the letter of the law was not as important as who held the power in any real-life situation. I could sue, but the suit would take several years and money I didn't have. The A.A.U.P. would investigate, and some years later would issue a report citing Spelman College for violating my academic freedom, but this would mean little. I soon concluded that I did not want to tie up my life with this fight. In doing so, I was reluctantly bowing to reality. "The rule of law" in such cases usually means that whoever can afford to pay lawyers and can afford to wait is the winner, and "justice" does not much matter.

The students were gone and scattered for the summer. But the news spread. Several who had become our close friends wrote or called to offer help. One was Betty Stevens, the student-body president, cool and indomitable (but she wept when she heard I was leaving); she would become the first Southern black woman to enter Harvard Law School. She wrote to President Manley: "Dr. Zinn's competence as a professor is unquestionable. . . . Dr. Zinn is admired, respected, and loved by all of the Spelman students. . . .

This man is not just a teacher, he is a friend to the students. He is someone that all students feel free to approach. . . . No person is insignificant to him." She ended her letter, "Disappointed in mankind."

(Being fired has some of the advantages of dying without its supreme disadvantage. People say extra-nice things about you, and you get to hear them.)

Another student who immediately gave her support was Alice Walker. I had first met Alice at an honors dinner for freshmen. We happened to be sitting next to one another at one of those long tables. I remember my first impression of her: small, slender but strong-looking, smooth brown skin, one eye silent, the other doubly inquiring with a hint of laughter. Her manner was polite, but not in the directed way of a "Spelman girl," rather almost ironically polite—not disrespectful, simply confident. We talked, and liked one another almost immediately.

She took my course in Russian history, was quiet in class but very attentive. I tried to liven the history by having students read Gogol, Chekhov, Dostoevsky, Tolstoy. Their first written essays came in, and I read with wonderment the one by Alice Walker, on Dostoevsky and Tolstoy. Not only had I never read a paper by an undergraduate written with such critical intelligence, but I had rarely read a literary essay of such grace and style by anyone. And she was nineteen, from a farm family in Eatonton, Georgia.

When Alice arrived at Spelman, a third wave of sit-ins and demonstrations was about to take place, and soon she was in the midst of it all.

Alice was a frequent visitor at our home and developed a wonderful rapport with our children. Her writing continued to dazzle me. When my letter of dismissal came in early June, Alice had already gone north to spend the summer with her brother in Boston. But someone called her with the news and she wrote to me immediately: "I've tried to imagine Spelman without you—and I can't at all. . . . Last night I was far too upset to finish my letter."

Roz and I went to Greenwood, Mississippi, that summer, where I was talking to movement people for my book on SNCC (the Student Nonviolent Coordinating Committee). By fall we were in Boston, where we had rented a house for the year, and I was weighing a job offer from Boston University.

Alice Walker was already planning to leave Spelman. She wrote to us from Atlanta: "There is nothing really here for me—it is almost like being buried alive. It seems almost a matter of getting away or losing myself—*my self*—in this strange, unreal place."

Sometime in October we took a trip back to Atlanta to arrange for the shipment of our belongings up to Boston and to see our friends. We visited the SNCC office and found it jammed with over a hundred Spelman students who had shown up to express their support. It was an emotional reunion.

It was those students and so many others who made the Spelman years, with all that turmoil—even with being fired—such a loving, wonderful time. Watching them change in those few years, seeing their spirit of defiance to established authority, off and on the campus, suggested the extraordinary possibilities in all human beings, of any race, in any time.

"My Name
Is Freedom":
Albany, Georgia

One day in the summer of 1962, as a thirty-nine-year-old professor of history who had begun to wander out of the classroom to see some history, I walked into the office of Sheriff Cull Campbell of Daugherty County, in the city of Albany, a city surrounded by the cotton and pecan land of southwest Georgia.

I was visiting Sheriff Campbell as part of an assignment I had undertaken for the Southern Regional Council, a liberal research group in Atlanta. In the winter of 1961 and the spring and summer of 1962, the black population of Albany, surprising itself and the world, rose up in rebellion against racial segregation. I was asked to look into the turmoil in Albany and write a report.

I wanted to talk with the sheriff because of something that had recently happened in his jurisdiction. A white civil rights worker named Bill Hansen, jailed with sixteen other people for praying in front of City Hall and refusing to move, had been put into a cell with a white prisoner who was given meaningful instructions: "This is one of those guys who came down here to straighten us out." As Hansen sat on the cell floor reading a newspaper he was attacked and beaten into unconsciousness, his jaw broken, his lip split, a number of ribs broken.

That same afternoon, a young lawyer, C. B. King, a native of Albany and the first black attorney in the history of the city, went into Sheriff Campbell's office to ask about what had happened to Bill Hansen. The sheriff was clearly infuriated by the sight of a black man, indeed a hometown "boy" who had grown up, gone to law school, and now appeared in suit and tie like any white lawyer, asking about a client. He said, "Nigger, haven't I told you to wait outside?" He then pulled a walking stick out of a basket and brought it down with all his force on King's head. The attorney staggered from the office, blood streaming down his face and onto his clothes, and made his way across the street to police chief Pritchett, who called for medical aid.

Sheriff Campbell, inviting me into his office a few weeks after that happened, turned and said, "You're not with the goddam niggers, are you?" I chose not to answer, but asked him about what happened to King. He stared at me. "Yeah, I knocked hell out of the son-of-a-bitch, and I'll do it again. I wanted to let him know . . . I'm a white man and he's a damn nigger."

As I listened to the sheriff I saw the basket of walking sticks near his desk. On it was a sign saying they were made by the blind and sold for fifty cents. I had a quick macabre vision of a black man in the county home for the blind making the cane that was used to beat C. B. King.

I walked across the street to Chief Pritchett's office. Pritchett had been hailed in newspapers all over the country for maintaining "order" in Albany. A reporter for the New York *Herald Tribune* said Pritchett "brought to Albany a standard of professional achievement that would be difficult to emulate in a situation so made to order for violence."

Pritchett earned this praise from the establishment press by simply putting into prison ("nonviolently," as he boasted) every man, woman, and child in the city of Albany who tried to exercise their constitutional rights of free speech and assembly. He and Sheriff Campbell were the classic bad cop–good cop team: Campbell would beat someone bloody and Pritchett would call for an ambulance.

I asked Pritchett why he did not arrest Sheriff Campbell, who was clearly guilty of assault. He smiled and said nothing. His secretary walked in. "Your next appointment is here." Pritchett stood up and shook my hand. I started to leave. His next appointment walked in: it was Dr. Martin Luther King. We greeted one another (we had met a number of times in Atlanta) and I left just as Pritchett—the good cop—shook hands cordially with King.

Back in my Albany motel room, starting to put together my report, I thought about all that had happened in the eight months since December of 1961:

Pritchett's arrest of SNCC workers who took the train to Albany from Atlanta and on arrival sat in the "white" waiting room. SNCC, the Student Nonviolent Coordinating Committee, was the newly formed organization composed mostly of young black college students who had been in the sit-ins all over the South the year before and now had decided to challenge racial segregation in the toughest, most violent regions of the country: Georgia, Alabama, Mississippi.

The arrest of four hundred black high school and college students who marched and sang downtown to protest the arrest of those SNCC "Freedom Riders."

The arrest of seventy more Albany blacks who knelt and prayed at City Hall.

The arrest of three hundred more who marched to City Hall; and two hundred and fifty more (this time including the recently arrived Martin Luther King, Jr.) who marched, singing, through downtown.

The arrest of even more people for sitting at lunch counters and refusing to leave until they were served.

Pritchett told reporters, "We can't tolerate the NAACP or the SNCC or any other nigger organization to take over this town with mass demonstrations."

In my report for the Southern Regional Council, I was searching for a central focus. Here, in concentrated form, was the racism, the brutality, of the segregated South. Just one instance: Mrs. Slater King (C. B. King's sister-in-law), with her three children and in her sixth month of pregnancy, tried to bring food to someone in jail. She was kicked and knocked to the ground by a deputy sheriff. She lost consciousness. Months later she lost her baby.

A question kept nagging at me: Where was the government of the United States in all this?

I taught courses in constitutional law, but that expertise was not necessary for a person to see that the First Amendment and Fourteenth Amendment rights in the United States Constitution were being violated in Albany again and again—freedom of speech, freedom of assembly, the equal protection of the law—I could count at least thirty such violations. Yet the president—sworn to uphold the Constitution—and all the agencies of the United States government at his disposal were nowhere to be seen. Was Albany, Georgia, was all of the South, outside the jurisdiction of the United States? Had the Confederacy really won the Civil War and morally, effectively seceded?

I knew that a post–Civil War law passed to enforce the Fourteenth Amendment made it a federal crime for any official to violate any citizen's constitutional rights. In the nation's capital a liberal Democratic administration had recently taken office. John F. Kennedy was president; Robert F. Kennedy was attorney general, head of the Justice Department, and therefore in charge of enforcing federal law. But this was not being done in Albany, Georgia.

My report to the Southern Regional Council became a front-page story in the *New York Times*. In it, I pointed to the failure of the national government in protecting constitutional rights. *I. F. Stone's Weekly* carried excerpts, and *The Nation* published an article of mine on the Albany events, entitled, "Kennedy, the Reluctant Emancipator."

Martin Luther King, Jr., was asked by the press if he agreed with the report. He said he did, pointing to racism in the FBI. This comment apparently enraged J. Edgar Hoover, the self-appointed "white knight" of patriotism, the anti-crime and anti-Communist "hero" of America, who was not accustomed to criticism. The press contributed to Hoover's fury by playing up the criticism of the FBI, but confined itself to that issue, while my report went beyond the FBI to the Justice Department and the White House. It was an example of a common phenomenon in American journalism (perhaps in social criticism in general), the shallow focusing on agents or on individuals, thus concealing what a deeper analysis would reveal—the failure of the government itself, indeed, of the political system.

At the great March on Washington of 1963, the chairman of the Student Nonviolent Coordinating Committee, John Lewis, speaking to the same enormous crowd that heard Martin Luther King's "I Have a Dream," was prepared to ask the right question: "Which side is the federal government on?" That sentence was eliminated from his speech by organizers of the march to avoid offending the Kennedy administration, but Lewis and his fellow SNCC workers had experienced, again and again, the strange passivity of the national government in the face of Southern violence—strange, considering how often this same government had been willing to intervene *outside* the country, often with overwhelming force.

John Lewis and SNCC had reason to be angry. John had been beaten bloody by a white mob in Montgomery as a Freedom Rider in the spring of 1961. The federal government had trusted the notoriously racist Alabama police to protect the riders, but done nothing itself except to have FBI agents take notes. Instead of insisting that blacks and whites had a right to ride the buses together, the Kennedy administration called for a "cooling-off period," a moratorium on Freedom Rides.

When the movement people insisted on continuing the rides into Mississippi, Attorney General Kennedy made a deal with the governor of Mississippi: the Freedom Riders would not be beaten, but they would be arrested. Some three hundred were, by the end of that summer, and spent hard time in Mississippi jails because the government of the United States did not see fit to protect their rights.

The Freedom Rides pushed the Justice Department into getting the Interstate Commerce Commission to issue regulations barring racial segregation on trains and in terminals, effective November 1, 1961. It was that order that SNCC people decided to test in the train terminal of Albany, Georgia. They were arrested and notified the Department of Justice, which, by its silence, then failed the test.

SNCC (known to its friends as "Snick") had been formed in the spring of 1960, when veterans of the recent sit-ins got together in Raleigh, North Carolina. Inspiring and overseeing its beginning was the extraordinary Ella Baker, veteran of struggles in Harlem and elsewhere. When Albany blacks turned out in the streets by the hundreds to protest the arrests of the Albany Freedom Riders, and were arrested themselves, Ella Baker was there. Months later, when SNCC asked me to join their executive committee as one of their two "adult advisers," along with Miss Baker (that's how movement people referred to her), I felt honored.

When I first arrived in Albany in December of 1961, hundreds of people were coming out of jail. Many of them had been fired by their white employers, and they gathered in the Shiloh Baptist Church for help. Ella Baker sat in a corner of the church, pen and paper in hand. She was a middle-aged, handsome woman with the resonant voice of a stage actress, who moved silently through the protest movements in the South, doing the things the famous men didn't have time to do. Now, hour after hour, she sat there as people lined up before her, patiently taking down names, addresses, occupations, immediate money needs.

I spoke to those sitting on a bench waiting to see Miss Baker. They described their prison experiences. One woman said, "We were eighty-eight in one room with twenty steel bunks and no mattresses. Sheriff took us to Camilla. On the bus he told us, 'We don't have no singin', no prayin', and no handclappin' here.'" A young married woman who was a student at Albany State College said, "I didn't expect to go to jail for kneeling and praying at City Hall."

The people I encountered in Albany in those days made me think of what stored-up courage and self-sacrifice one finds in so many people who never make the headlines but represent millions.

I think of Ola Mae Quarterman, eighteen years old, who took a front seat on a city bus and refused to move. She said, in language that was apparently new to the black-white culture of Albany, "I paid my damn twenty cents and I can sit where I want." She was arrested for "obscenity."

I think of Charles Sherrod. He was a SNCC "field secretary" and one of those young people who went into the toughest towns in the deep South to set up Freedom Houses and help local folk organize to change their lives. Sherrod was a Freedom Rider, jailed in Mississippi. Now he and Cordell Reagon, another SNCC fellow, went into Albany to see what they could do. (Yes, they were "outside agitators"—what great social movement ever did without such people?) Sherrod told me, "I remembered walking dusty roads for weeks without food. I remembered staying up all night for two and three nights in succession writing and cutting stencils and mimeographing and wondering, How long?" Sherrod was one of those just out of jail when I arrived in Albany. When he told the sheriff, "We may be in jail, but we're still human beings," the sheriff hit him in the face. (Twenty five years later the sheriff was gone, but Sherrod was still in Albany, organizing farming cooperatives.)

I think of Lenore Taitt, one of the eight Freedom Riders into Albany whose arrest had sparked all the demonstrations. She was one of my students at Spelman —a delightful young woman, far from the sober agitator of myth—a happy Freedom Rider of unquenchable spirit. I walked downtown to the county jail, a small stone building surrounded by a barbed wire fence, and asked to see her. Can't be done, said the deputy sheriff on duty. "You can holler through the fence like everyone else does." I shouted Lenore's name at a thick steel mesh window, impossible to see through, and then I heard Lenore's voice, incredibly hoarse. She explained that she'd lost it yelling all night to get help for a woman in her cell who was sick.

I think of Bob Zellner, one of the few white field secretaries in SNCC, from the Gulf coast of Alabama, who was arrested with Lenore Taitt and the other Freedom Riders. I was with the crowd waiting to greet them when they all came out of jail, but as Bob emerged with them, the sheriff grabbed him. "We've got another charge against *you*." Bob flashed his indomitable grin and waved to his friends as he was taken away.

Bob told me later that he'd had two books with him in jail. One was Henry Miller's *Tropic of Cancer*, which the sheriff glanced at and let him keep; the other was Lillian Smith's novel about a black man and a white woman, and the sheriff took it away, saying, "This is *obscene*."

And there was Stokely Carmichael, whom I first met in Albany on a steamy-hot night, sitting on the steps outside a church where a meeting was going on, a small group of neighborhood kids gathered around him. He gave the impression he would stride cool and smiling through hell, philosophizing all the way. He had left Howard University to join the Freedom Rides and was jailed on arrival in Jackson, Mississippi, making his way past a mob of howling, cursing people who threw lighted cigarettes at him. In Parchman State Prison he drove his captors crazy with his defiance, and they were relieved when after forty-nine days he was out. Now he was in Albany for SNCC.

And Bernice Johnson, who organized the Albany Freedom Singers and was expelled from Albany State College for her determined involvement in the movement. I helped her get into Spelman College, but both the college and its famous glee club were too narrow to contain her spirit and her voice. She sat in our living room one day to tell us this, and then sang, with that magnificent deep voice. (Later, she would get a Ph.D. in history, but that does not begin to suggest her power. She would become an indefatigable curator of oral history at the Smithsonian, inspire countless audiences, and sing at Carnegie Hall and all over the country with her group Sweet Honey in the Rock.)

There was the Albany youngster who was in the line of black people being booked at the City Hall after a protest parade.

"How old are you?" Chief Pritchett asked.

"Nine."

"What is your name?" asked the chief.

The boy answered. "Freedom. Freedom."

The chief said, "Go home, Freedom."

IT HAS OFTEN BEEN SAID, by journalists, by scholars, that Albany, Georgia, was a defeat for the movement, because there was no immediate victory over racial segregation in the city. That always seemed to me a superficial assessment, a mistake often made in evaluating protest movements. Social movements may have many "defeats"—failing to achieve objectives in the short run—but in the course of the struggle the strength of the old order begins to erode, the minds of people begin to change; the protesters are momentarily defeated but not crushed, and have been lifted, heartened, by their ability to fight back. The boy may have been sent home by Chief Pritchett, but he was a different boy than he had been a month before. Albany was changed forever by the tumultuous events of 1961 and 1962, however much things *looked* the same when the situation quieted down.

The white population could not possibly be unaffected by those events—some whites perhaps more stubborn in their defense of segregation, but others beginning to think in different ways. And the black population was certainly transformed, having risen up in mass action for the first time, feeling its power, knowing that if the old order could be shaken, it could be toppled.

Indeed, in 1976, fifteen years after he arrived and was arrested, Charles Sherrod was elected to the Albany city commission. He responded to the pessimists, "Some people talk about failure. Where's the failure? Are we not integrated in every facet? Did we stop at any time? Did any injunction stop us? Did any white man stop us? Did any black man stop us? Nothing stopped us in Albany, Georgia. We showed the world."

What black men, women, children did in Albany at that time was heroic. They overcame a century of passivity, and they did it without the help of the national government. They learned that despite the Constitution, despite the promises, despite the political rhetoric of the government, whatever they accomplished in the future would have to come from them.

One day I drove out of Albany, from dirt road onto dirt road, deep into Lee County to talk to James Mays, a teacher and a farmer.

The night before, thirty bullets had been fired into his house, crashing into the walls and barely missing the sleeping children inside.

He knew there was no point in making a call to the Department of Justice. Many, many calls had been made. When dawn came he lettered a sign of protest and stood with it, alone, on the main road to the county seat. It was clear that although he was a citizen of a nation whose power stretched around the globe and into space, that power was absent for him. He and his people were on their own.

For an aggrieved group to learn that it must rely on itself, even if the learning is accompanied by bitter losses in the immediate sense, is to strengthen itself for future struggles. The spirit of defiance that appeared in Albany in that time of turmoil was to outlast the momentary "defeat" that the press and the pundits lamented so myopically.

That spirit is epitomized by eighteen-year-old Ola Mae Quarterman: "I paid my damn twenty cents and I'll sit where I please."

Selma, Alabama

I traveled to Selma, Alabama, in October 1963 as an adviser to SNCC, to observe its voter registration campaign there, which had been accompanied by a number of acts of intimidation and violence. The town was the seat of Dallas County, whose population was 57-percent black, with 1 percent of those registered to vote. (Sixty-four percent of whites were registered.)

The 1 percent figure was understandable when you looked at the registration process. You didn't register, you applied to register. There was a long questionnaire, then an oral examination, with different questions for blacks and whites. A typical question for blacks: "Summarize the Constitution of the United States." (The county registrar was undoubtedly an expert on the Constitution.) Later, a postcard saying if you passed or failed.

Selma was a slave market before the Civil War, a lynching town at the turn of the century, and by the 1960s still a place where any young black person growing up there had to say to himself or herself, as a Selma-born black attorney living in Tennessee told me, "I must get out of this town."

Not long before I arrived, thirty-two schoolteachers who had tried to register to vote had been fired, and John Lewis had been arrested for leading a picket line at the county courthouse. (Only one of his many arrests and brutal beatings. In the 1980s, he would be elected to the U.S. Congress from Georgia.) Worth Long, another SNCC man, was arrested and beaten by a deputy sheriff in the county jail. A nineteen-year-old girl was knocked off a stool in a store and prodded with an electric pole as she lay on the floor unconscious. Bernard Lafayette, a SNCC field organizer whose job was to try to register black voters, was clubbed as he stopped on the street to help a white man who said his car needed a push.

My experience in Albany had made me especially conscious of the federal role in keeping the institutions of racism going. A systematic failure to enforce civil rights law had marked every national administration since 1877, whether Democrat or Republican, liberal or conservative. Racism was not southern policy, it was national policy. Selma was an *American* city.

Still, there was something unreal about Selma. It was as if a Hollywood producer had reconstructed a pre–Civil War Southern town—decaying buildings, muddy streets, little cafes, and a mule drawing a wagonload of cotton down the street. In the midst of that, startlingly, the huge red brick Hotel Albert, modeled after a medieval Venetian palace.

In every such Southern town I visited there seemed to be one black family that was the rock-like center of any freedom movement. In Selma it was the family of Mrs. Amelia Boynton. In her home I spoke to three young local fellows. "Do you know any white man in Selma—just one even—who is sympathetic with your cause?" They thought there might be one Jewish storekeeper who was secretly sympathetic, but knew only one white man who openly helped the movement. This was a thirty-seven-year-old Catholic priest, Father Maurice Ouillet, in charge of the St. Edmonds Mission in Selma, who had received abusive phone calls and warnings he might be killed.

SNCC had declared October 7 as Freedom Day. The idea was to bring hundreds of people to register to vote, hoping that their numbers would decrease fear. And there was much to fear. John Lewis and seven others were still in jail. Sheriff Jim Clark, huge and bullying, had deputized a force that was armed and on the prowl. To build up courage, people gathered in churches night after night before Freedom Day. The churches were packed as people listened to speeches, prayed, sang.

Two nights before Freedom Day, I went to a crowded church meeting to hear Dick Gregory, who had just arrived in Selma; his wife Lillian had been arrested while demonstrating there. Armed deputies ringed the church outside. Three white police officers sat in the audience taking notes, and Gregory was determined to speak about them and to them in a manner unheard of in Selma—to show that it was possible to speak to white people insubordinately.

I traveled in those days with a cheap tape recorder. (I had written to my alma mater, Columbia University, which had an oral history project, suggesting that they take time off from interviewing ex–generals and ex–secretaries of state and send someone south to record the history being made every day by obscure people. One of the nation's richest universities wrote back saying something like, "An excellent idea. We don't really have the resources.") I recorded Gregory's performance with my little machine.

He spoke for two hours, lashing out at white Southern society with passion and with his extraordinary wit. Never in the history of this area had a black man stood like this on a public platform ridiculing and denouncing white officials to their faces. The crowd loved it and applauded wildly again and again. He spoke of the irony of whites' maltreatment of black people, whose labor they depended on for their lives. He said he wished that the whole Negro race would disappear overnight—"They would go crazy looking for us!" The crowd roared and applauded.

Then Gregory lowered his voice, suddenly serious. "But it looks like we got to do it the hard way, and stay down here, and educate them."

After him, Jim Forman spoke. He was the executive director of SNCC, working in the Atlanta office, but moving onto the firing line again and again with an awesome quiet bravery. He was Chicago born, but grew up in Mississippi, spent four years in the Air Force, was a college graduate. Now he set about organizing the people in the church for Freedom Day. "All right, let's go through the phone book. . . . You take a baloney sandwich and a glass of cool water and go down there and stay all day." He pointed to the big sign up on the platform: DO YOU WANT TO BE FREE? He paused. "Who'll take the letter *A*?"

The evening ended with the Selma Freedom Chorus, including some small children, some teenagers, and a boy at the piano—the most beautiful singing I had heard since the mass meetings in Albany. (That is something impossible to convey in words—the singing, the ever-present singing—in churches, at staff meetings, everywhere, raising the emotional level, giving people courage, almost always ending with everyone, knowing one another or not, holding hands.)

Then everyone went home, through the doors out into the street, where two cars with white men had been sitting all evening in the darkness outside the church.

Some of us waited that night at Mrs. Boynton's for James Baldwin to arrive. He was flying into Birmingham to be driven by SNCC people to Selma, coming to observe Freedom Day. While waiting, we sat around in the kitchen and talked. Jim Forman expertly scrambled eggs in a frying pan with one hand, gesturing with the other to make a point.

Baldwin arrived after midnight, his brother David with him. We all sat in the living room and waited for him to say something. He smiled broadly. "You fellows talk. I'm new here. I'm trying to find out what's happening."

I made notes on Freedom Day, almost minute by minute, starting at 9:30 in the morning, standing on the street near the Dallas County courthouse as the line of black people grew into the hundreds. The editor of the local newspaper told me that the application process was slow. I calculated that at the rate it was going it would take ten years for blacks to catch up to whites in percentage of registered voters.

By 11:00 A.M. there were two hundred and fifty people in the line, which extended the full length of the block, around the corner, and halfway down that street. Standing guard over these people—including elderly men and women, young mothers carrying babies in their arms—were helmeted men with clubs and guns, members of Sheriff Jim Clark's posse. The sheriff was there, a six-footer with a big belly, on his green helmet the confederate flag and a gold medallion with an eagle, a gold star on his shirt, epaulets on his shoulders, gun at his hip.

Directly across the street from the county courthouse in Selma was the federal building. On the first floor of that building was the office of the FBI, its windows looking out at the county courthouse. Standing on the street, witnessing everything that happened that day, were four FBI agents and two lawyers from the Justice Department, one white, one black.

By 11:40 A.M. no one could find a black person who had come out of the courthouse who had actually gone through the registration procedure. I was standing with Jim Forman and another SNCC man when Sheriff Clark came over. "All right, clear out of here. You're blocking the sidewalk."

A man with sound equipment spoke to James Baldwin, whose eyes looked enormous, fiery. Baldwin waved toward the line of helmeted troopers. "The federal government is not doing what it is supposed to do."

It was almost noon, the sun was beating down, and Forman was musing about the problem of getting water to the people on line, who had been standing there almost three hours. I looked across the street to the federal building. There on the steps were two SNCC fellows holding signs that faced the registration line. One of them, in overalls and fedora, had a sign saying, "REGISTER TO VOTE."

I moved across the street to get a better look. As I did so, Sheriff Clark and three helmeted deputies came walking fast across the street. They went past the two Justice Department attorneys and two FBI men, up the steps of the building, and grabbed the two SNCC men. Clark called out, "You're under arrest for unlawful assembly." The deputies pulled the two down the steps and pushed them into a police car. A third man at the side entrance to the building, also holding a voter registration sign, was also arrested.

There could hardly be a more clear-cut violation of the 1957 Civil Rights Act, which prohibits interference with the right to vote—to say nothing of the First Amendment's right to free speech. And this had taken place on the steps of the U.S. government's building, before the eyes of government men. I turned to the Justice Department man near me. "Is that a *federal* building?" I asked with some anger. "Yes," he said, and turned away. The police car with the three SNCC men sped off.

Jim Forman told me that the night before he had wired the Justice Department for federal marshals, sure there would be trouble. The Justice Department had not replied.

Word came that the registrars had stopped registering for the lunch period. People stayed on the line and Forman began planning how to get food to them. A caravan of state troopers had arrived at the courthouse. Their autos were lined up along the curb from one end of the street to the other, searchlights mounted on top. Forty troopers, with blue helmets, clubs, and guns, stationed themselves alongside the registration line. In charge of the troopers was Colonel Al Lingo, the veteran bully of Birmingham. Some of his men were holding electric cattle prods.

At 1:55 p.m. (people had now been on line five hours), Jim Forman and Mrs. Boynton walked over to talk to Sheriff Clark.

Forman said, "Sheriff, we'd like to give these people some food."

Clark replied, "They will not be molested in any way."

Forman said, "We don't want to molest them. We want to give them food and to talk to them about registration."

Now Clark began shouting. "If you do, you'll be arrested! They will not be molested in any way and that includes talking to them."

Forman and Mrs. Boynton went back across the street, to the alley alongside the federal building, where a shopping cart with sandwiches and a keg of water was set up. Newsmen were called over. Forman told them about his wire to the Justice Department and their silence. Mrs. Boynton said, "We're determined to reach these people on line with food."

At 2:00 P.M. I looked up at the windows of the county court-house and saw the faces of county employees jammed up against the glass.

I spoke to the senior Justice Department attorney. "Is there any reason why a representative of the Justice Department can't go over and talk to the state troopers and say these people are entitled to food and water?"

He seemed agitated by the question. There was a long pause. Then he said, "I won't do it." He paused again. "I believe they do have the right to receive food and water. But I won't do it. It's no use. Washington won't stand by me."

Two SNCC field secretaries stood before the shopping cart and filled their arms with food. One of them was Avery Williams, Alabama born; another was Chico Neblett from Carbondale, Illinois. Both had left college to work for SNCC.

Chico gave his wallet to Forman—a final small acceptance of going to jail. He said to Avery, "Let's go, man."

They walked down to the corner and crossed (SNCC people took care not to jaywalk in the South) with all eyes on the street focused on them. A group of us—photographers, newsmen, others—crossed the street at the same time. It was 2:20 P.M.

As Chico and Avery came close to the line, a bulky trooper with cigar and blue helmet (he had been identified to us as Major Smelley) barked at them (Am I being unfair? Is there a kinder verb?). "Move on!" They kept going toward the line of registrants.

The major called out, "Get 'em!" The next thing I saw was Chico Neblett on the ground, troopers all around him. I heard him cry out and saw his body jump convulsively again and again. They were jabbing him and Avery with their cattle prods. Then they lifted them by their arms and legs and threw them into the green arrest truck that stood at the curb.

Now the troopers and deputies turned on the group of us who had followed all this, pushing and shoving us to prevent pictures being taken. There was a young reporter for the *Montgomery Advertiser* with a camera. They smashed it with a billy club, pinned him against a parked truck, and ripped his shirt, and then a deputy backhanded him across the mouth. This was a military operation and national security demanded secrecy.

The green arrest truck pulled away. Chico and Avery waved. The Justice Department attorney took the name of the photographer who had been hit. James Baldwin and I went into the FBI office to talk to the chief. Baldwin was angry, upset. I asked, "Why didn't you arrest Sheriff Clark and the others for violating federal law?" (After my Albany experience I could cite the law, Section 242, Title 18 of the U.S. Code: "Whoever, under color of any law . . . or custom, willfully subjects . . . any inhabitant . . . to the deprivation of any rights . . . secured or protected by the Constitution . . . shall be fined . . . or imprisoned.")

The FBI chief looked at us. "We don't have the right to make arrests in these circumstances." It was an absurd statement. Section 3052, Title 18 of the U.S. Administrative Code gives FBI agents the power to make arrests without warrants "for any offense against the United States committed in their presence." The FBI makes arrests in kidnappings, bank robberies, drug cases, espionage cases. But not in civil rights cases? Then not only were black people second-class citizens, but civil rights law was second-class law.

Four of us sat on the steps of the federal building and talked: James Baldwin, myself, the senior attorney from the Justice Department, and a young black attorney from Detroit who had come to observe Freedom Day. The Detroit attorney said, "Those cops could have massacred all those three hundred Negroes on line, and still nothing would have been done." The Justice man was defensive. He asked Baldwin what he was working on now. Answer: a play. What was the title? "Blues for Mister Charlie," Baldwin replied.

At 4:30 P.M. the county courthouse closed its doors. The line was breaking up. The Detroit attorney watched men and women walk slowly away. His voice trembled. "Those people should be given medals." We made our way back to SNCC headquarters.

(Years later, I was in the House of Representatives office building in Washington. Near the elevator I ran into the lawyer from Detroit. "What are you doing here?" he asked. "The Vietnam War,"

I answered. "What about you?" He smiled. "I've just been elected to Congress." This was John Conyers, who in the years to come would be one of the stalwarts for justice and against war, as a member of the Congressional Black Caucus.)

A mass meeting was called for 8:00 P.M. at a church. At five minutes of eight the church was packed, every seat taken, people standing along the walls. Father Ouillet and another Catholic priest sat in the audience. A chandelier hung way up in the domed ceiling, a circle of twenty-five bare light bulbs glowing. A seventy-three-year-old man, a veteran of World War I, told me, "Nothing like this ever happened to Selma. Nothing—until SNCC came here."

Jim Forman told the crowd, "We ought to be happy today, because we did something great." There was bitterness that unarmed black people of Dallas County had to defend the Constitution themselves, against Jim Clark and his posse, with no help from the United States government. But there was exultation that three hundred and fifty of them had stood on line from morning to evening, without food or water, in full view of the armed men who ruled Dallas County, and had not flinched.

The young people in the chorus were up front, singing. "Oh, that light of fre-ee-dom, I'm gonna let it shine!"

James Baldwin stood at the rostrum, his eyes burning into the crowd. "The sheriff and his deputies . . . were created by the good white people on the hill—and in Washington—and they've created a monster they can't control. . . . It's not an act of God. It is deliberately done, deliberately created by the American Republic."

The meeting closed as always, with everyone linking arms and singing "We Shall Overcome," youngsters and old people and young women holding their babies, the SNCC people and the Catholic priests. Over on the other side of the church I saw the young black Justice Department attorney, his arms crossed like everyone else, singing.

I wrote up a short account of Freedom Day for the *New Republic*, which they headed, "Registration in Alabama: Negroes Are Dragged off Federal Property as the FBI Looks On." The Justice Department was not happy with my piece. The chief of its Civil

Rights Division, Burke Marshall, wrote a long letter to the *New Republic*, saying that "litigation" was the proper remedy for what happened in Selma and that the Justice Department had two voting rights suits pending in Selma. He said there could be "no summary action." (Marshall chose to ignore, as the FBI chief had done, the arrest powers of FBI agents, which could be invoked "for any offense" committed in their presence.)

A year or so later, Marshall wrote a small book in which he elaborated his defense of federal inaction in such cases as Selma. He talked about the "federal system," with its division of powers between nation and states. It was an astounding argument, as if the Fourteenth Amendment had not permanently altered that division, giving the federal government enormous power to act when local officials failed to protect constitutional rights. Section 333, Title 10 of the U.S. Code made this power clear.

I received in the mail one day a copy of the *University of Chicago Law Review*, and in it was a review of Marshall's book. It was a devastating critique of his reasoning by a law professor named Richard Wasserstrom. I was startled—and pleased. Richard Wasserstrom was the Justice Department lawyer I had met in Selma that day. I learned that he had quit the department after the Selma events, become a dean at Tuskegee Institute in Alabama, and was now a professor of law and philosophy at the University of California. Around the same time, I heard that the black Justice Department attorney I had met in Selma and who joined in singing "We Shall Overcome" had also left the department.

That was not my last experience in Selma. In early 1965, Selma became a national scandal, and an international embarrassment for the Johnson administration. Demonstrations against racial segregation were met with mass arrests, the clubbing to death of a white Unitarian Universalist minister named James Reeb, the shooting of a black man, Jimmie Lee Jackson, and the bloody beating of blacks trying to march across a bridge out of Selma toward the state capital of Montgomery.

Finally, Johnson asked Congress to pass a strong voting rights act, and ordered a federalized Alabama National Guard to protect the planned civil rights walk from Selma to Montgomery. It would be a fifty-mile trek, a triumphant march after all the beatings, all the bloodshed.

I was writing an article for the hundredth-anniversary issue of *The Nation*, based on the idea of revisiting the South a century after the end of the Civil War, and so I traveled to Lynchburg, Virginia, John's Island, South Carolina, and Vicksburg, Mississippi. Then I joined the Selma to Montgomery march for its final eighteen miles to the Alabama capital.

Arriving the night before, I found the marchers settling down just off the main highway. It had rained hard that day, and the field chosen to serve as our camp for the night was a bed of pure mud so deep your shoes went into it up to the ankles.

We were given plastic sheets and sleeping bags. I lay down in the darkness, listened to the hum of portable generators, and watched as people coming off the main highway were checked by two husky "security" men, young Episcopalian priests with turned-around collars who carried walkie-talkies.

The plastic sheet under me was soaked in mud and slime, but the inside of the sleeping bag was dry. Two hundred feet away, in a great arc around the field, were fires lit by soldiers on guard through the night. It was hard to believe—the movement was finally getting the federal protection it had asked for.

I awoke just before dawn, with a half-moon pushing through the clouds. The soldiers' fires at the perimeter were low now, but still burning. Nearby, sleepers were beginning to awaken.

A line formed for hot oatmeal, hard-boiled eggs, coffee. Then everyone gathered to resume the march. A black girl washed her bare feet, then her sneakers, in a stream alongside the road. Near her was a minister, his coat streaked with mud. A black woman without shoes had her feet wrapped in plastic. Andy Young was calling over the main transmitter to Montgomery. "Get us some shoes. We need forty pairs of shoes, all sizes, for women and kids. They've been walking barefoot the past twenty-four hours."

At exactly 7:00 A.M., an Army helicopter fluttered overhead and the march began, down to the main highway and on to Montgomery, with Martin Luther King and Andy Young and some SNCC people in the lead. On both sides of the march, as far forward and back as you could see, there were soldiers.

I was walking next to Eric Weinberger, a legendary pacifist, a veteran of torture in Southern jails, of beatings and cattle prods, who once fasted thirty-one days in jail. As Eric and I walked along, he pointed to the soldiers guarding the march. "Do you agree with that?" he asked.

"Yes, I'm glad they're there," I said. I understood his point. He was holding steady to pacifist-anarchist principle: do not use the instruments of the state, even on your behalf; do not use coercion, even against violent racists. But I was not an absolutist on the use of the state if, under popular pressure, it became a force for good. We agreed to disagree.

With the sun shining beautifully overhead, the marchers sang. "Free*dom*! Free*dom*! Freedom's coming and it won't be long." Of course it would be long, but did that matter if people were on the move, knowing they were shortening the distance however long it was?

It was seventeen miles to the edge of Montgomery, the original straggling line of three hundred thickening by the hour as thousands joined, whites and blacks who had come from all over the country. There was sunshine most of the way, then three or four bursts of drenching rain. On the porch of a cabin set way back from the road, eight tiny black children stood in a line and waved, an old hobby horse in the front yard.

A red-faced portly Irishman, newly arrived from Dublin, wearing a trench coat, held the hand of a little black boy who walked barefoot next to him. A Greyhound bus rode past with black kids on the way to school. They leaned out the window, shouting, "Freedom!" A one-legged young white man on crutches, a black skullcap over his red hair, marched along quickly with the rest.

A group of white workingmen along the road watched silently. As we reached the outskirts of Montgomery, students poured out of a black high school, lined the streets, and waved and sang as the marchers went by. A jet plane zoomed close overhead and everyone stretched arms to the sky, shouting, "FREEDOM! FREEDOM!"

Once in the city, I left the march. I knew there would be a wonderful gathering at the capitol and a huge crowd, which King and others would address, but I wanted to get home. I made my way to the airport, and ran into Whitney Young, my old Atlanta University colleague, now head of the National Urban League. He was coming off a plane to join the celebration.

Whitney and I went into the airport cafeteria and sat down at a table to have a cup of coffee. We weren't sure if that would work. And we must have looked odd together, not just because of the difference in race, but because Whitney, tall and handsome as always, was in a dark suit, white shirt, and tie, and I was quite bedraggled, unshaven, my clothes still splattered with mud from the march.

The woman who came to wait on our table looked us over. She was not happy. I saw that on her apron she wore a huge button with the one word that had become the defiant slogan of the segregationists: NEVER! But something had changed in Alabama, because she brought us our coffee. Obviously, although the marchers' song was not quite true ("Freedom's coming and it won't be long"), the claim on the button was now certainly false.

1 2 3 4 5 **6** 7 8 9 10 11 12 13 14 15

"I'll Be Here": Mississippi

By the time Roz and I traveled to Greenwood, Mississippi, in the summer of 1963, SNCC had worked in the state for two years. But the word "work" does not begin to convey the reality. Mississippi was known to black people as a killing state.

Bob Moses gave me a rundown. I had my little tape recorder with me; I had just agreed to write a book on SNCC for Beacon Press in Boston. (They had originally asked me to do one on the NAACP. I said, "No, the real story in the South today is SNCC.") I had begun to understand, back in Albany and Selma, how so much of what is called history omits the reality of ordinary people—their struggles, their hidden power.

Bob was a twenty-nine-year-old college graduate from Harlem who went South to be with SNCC, moved into Mississippi, and started to work with local black people, mostly to help them register to vote. I described him in my book on SNCC as "of medium height and sturdy build, with light brown skin and a few freckles near his nose, who looks at you directly out of large tranquil eyes, who talks slowly, quietly, whose calm as he stands looking down a street in Mississippi is that of a mountain studying the sea."

The prospect of black people voting made the white power structure of the state very nervous. Blacks were 43 percent of the population, but because only 5 percent were registered to vote they had zero political power, and the establishment wanted to keep it that way. A small number of whites controlled the wealth of the state, using a tiny part of this wealth to pay the salaries of thousands of petty local officials who kept the system as it was, by force if necessary.

So when Bob Moses began to talk to people in Mississippi, starting in the little town of McComb in the southern part of the state, he was at different times jailed, beaten, knifed, and threatened with death. When two eighteen-year-old fellows sat in at the Woolworth lunch counter in McComb—the first such act of defiance in the history of the area—they were arrested and sentenced to thirty days in jail. When six high school students, led by fifteen-year-old Brenda Travis, did the same, they were sentenced to eight months in jail, and she was expelled from school.

Bob had not been in Mississippi long when he was called upon to examine the body of a farmer named Herbert Lee, father of nine children, who had been shot to death by a white man. They had been arguing. The white man had walked up to him and fired a pistol into his head. A coroner's jury acquitted the killer after a black witness, afraid for his own life, testified that it was self-defense. Weeks later the witness decided to tell the truth, and he was killed in his front yard by three shotgun blasts.

In protest against these incidents, over a hundred high school students in McComb stayed out of school. The jailings and beatings continued, but the black people of McComb had begun to act to change their lives.

After McComb, Bob Moses, joined by other SNCC people, decided to go north into the Mississippi Delta, spreading out into various towns. The city of Greenwood in Leflore County became a special focus of attention. The Delta became a war zone.

Sam Block was one of its unarmed soldiers. He was twenty-three, tall, gaunt, from a small town in Mississippi, son of a construction worker. Sam liked to sing, but not to speak much. Nevertheless, he did start walking through the black section of Greenwood, knocking on doors, talking to people about what their needs were. A police car followed him around as he did this, so folks began to be afraid to open their doors. One day, three white men pounced on him and beat him up; another day he had to jump behind a telephone pole to escape a speeding truck that tried to run him down.

Sam took up the cause of a fourteen-year-old boy who had been picked up by police and charged with burglary. The boy said he was innocent, that he had worked all day in the cotton fields on the day of the burglary, but the police took him to the police station, stripped him, threw him onto a concrete floor, used a bullwhip on his naked body, and beat him with fists, a billy club, and a blackjack. Sam took affidavits from the boy and photos of his wounds, and sent them all to the Justice Department in Washington. It was like dropping them into a bottomless, bucketless well. "From then on," Bob Moses told me, "it was Sam versus the police."

Sam Block's courage was contagious. More people began to show up at the SNCC office in Greenwood, and to go to the county courthouse to register to vote. One night Sam and two other SNCC workers, working late in the office, narrowly escaped a group of intruders armed with guns and chains by climbing through the window and across to a neighboring roof. They returned to the office the next day to find it a shambles.

But Sam kept on. That winter he was mostly busy collecting food for hungry people. There were twenty-two thousand people in the county who had depended on government surplus food, which the county had stopped distributing.

Taking some black people one day to register in Greenwood, Sam Block was stopped by the sheriff and their conversation (overheard by another SNCC worker) went like this:

SHERIFF: Nigger, where you from?
BLOCK: I'm a native of Mississippi.
SHERIFF: I know all the niggers here.
BLOCK: Do you know any colored people? (The sheriff spat at him.)
SHERIFF: I'll give you till tomorrow to get out of here.
BLOCK: If you don't want to see me here, you better pack up and leave, because I'll be here.

The war continued, with shotgun blasts into the homes of black people and into parked cars, with thirteen 45-calibre bullets fired into a car in which Bob Moses was riding with SNCC man Jimmy Travis, who was shot in the shoulder and neck and came close to death. When, after one of the shootings, a hundred black men, women, children, singing and praying, marched toward the Leflore County Courthouse, the police appeared wearing yellow helmets, carrying riot sticks, leading police dogs. One of the dogs attacked Bob Moses, and Marian Wright, who was on the scene, told later of how Bob was afraid of dogs but refused to move away, kept walking toward the dogs.

When Roz and I came to Greenwood in that summer of 1963, fifty-eight people had just been released from jail after a protest march against police brutality; they'd been freed on bond money supplied by the National Council of Churches. That night, SNCC headquarters had the eerie quality of a field hospital after a battle. Youngsters out of jail—sixteen and seventeen years old—were sprawled here and there. Two of them lay on narrow cots while a few of the SNCC girls dabbed their eyes with boric acid solutions; some dietary deficiency in jail had affected their eyes. One boy nursed an infected hand. Another boy's foot was swollen. He had been in the "hot box" at Parchman Penitentiary. Medical attention had been refused them in prison.

A youngster named Fred Harris told about it: "I spent a hundred and sixty hours in the hole—the hot box, that is. . . . I'm seventeen. I got involved with the movement back in 1960. I was fourteen then. Sam Block was talking to me about the movement. I told him yes, I'd be glad to help. . . . At first my mother didn't want me to

be in it. Then she realized it would be best for her and for me. . . .
She told me I could go ahead."

There was a woman living next door to the SNCC headquarters
in Greenwood who, people said, had been wonderfully helpful—
Mrs. Ruby Pilcher. Roz and I arranged to see her. We sat in her
kitchen and I set up my little recorder while she ironed clothes and
talked about her life, her work, her family, her feelings about the
movement.

She worked at the country club in Greenwood. "Well, I help the
cook and then we waits on the people, you know. Set tables, pick
up dishes, you know, just anything. . . . I had been hearing it
talked around, you know [voter registration]. . . . One morning
they said, you know, they burned the office up there where the
outside agitators had an office. . . . We didn't know what to
think. . . .

"Didn't know what to say about it because it was just something
that was happening here that never had happened before. And me,
myself, just going along working for the white people, taking what
little they put on us, doing just whatever we had to do. I never had
given a thought about freedom. And I was wondering what did it
mean about freedom, you know. . . .

"They went to giving out food over here in a church. Polices
went over there and arrested them. . . . I was afraid. . . . A man
named Dick Gregory—was that his name?—he come up here too.
So he said that he was going to lead the marches. . . . Yes, I went
to the mass meeting. And he told a lady that night, an old lady who
lives right up the street here . . . to lead the line with him. And he
said, 'Well, you be there at 7:00 A.M.' She said, 'I can get there at
6:00.'"

She showed us a photo of her two boys and two girls. "My girl
is seventeen. She has been just scared out, you know, of the movement. . . . Now she likes it. She said, 'Mama, I really like what is
going on and I hope it will be one day.'

"I just love the movement, so . . . anything we could do to help
the movement, you know, we thought it is right. . . . And we

would do that, we would neglect things for ourselves, let them have it, you know, do without. . . . They didn't have a stove out there, anything to make coffee, you know. And it was so cold that morning . . . I said, 'Well, after I finish making you some coffee I will make some biscuits, . . . lots of them.'"

It was always interesting to me how people got involved in the movement. How so often it was some small encounter, the tiniest of experiences, activating a lifetime of stored-up feeling.

Some months after our visit to Greenwood, I was at a SNCC staff meeting in Greenville and spoke to a forty-seven-year-old mother of two who had all her life been a sharecropper in Ruleville, Mississippi. She was short and stocky, her skin like weather-beaten copper, her eyes soft and large. She walked with a limp because she'd had polio as a child. This was Mrs. Fannie Lou Hamer.

She sang beautifully, and when she told me how she got into the movement she interspersed her conversation with song. She had heard about a meeting at a church in Ruleville. "James Bevel did talk that night, and everything he said, you know, made sense. And also, Jim Forman was there. So when they stopped talking, well, they wanted to know who would go down to register, you see, on this particular Friday, and I held up my hand.

"The thirty-first of August in '62—the day I went into the courthouse to register—well, after I'd gotten back home this man that I had worked for as a timekeeper and sharecropper for eighteen years, he said that I would just have to leave. . . . So I told him I wasn't trying to register for him, I was trying to register for myself. . . . I didn't have no other choice because for one time I wanted things to be different."

She was evicted from the plantation and moved in with a friend. Ten days later, a car drove by the house and sixteen bullets were pumped into the bedroom where she slept. That night she happened to be elsewhere, and no one was hurt.

Mrs. Hamer told me that a few months earlier she and five other movement people had been returning to Greenwood from a meeting in South Carolina. The bus stopped briefly in Winona, Mississippi, and some of them went into the "white" waiting room. They were all arrested, taken to jail, separated from one another. Annelle Ponder, a graduate of Clark College in Atlanta (her younger sister was a student of mine at Spelman), was beaten to the point where her face was so swollen she could barely speak. Mrs. Hamer was beaten with blackjacks all over her body.

She reflected, "You know they said outsiders was coming in and beginning to get the people stirred up because they've always been satisfied. Well, as long as I can remember, I've never been satisfied." I asked her if she was going to remain with the movement and she responded with the words to a song: "I told them if they ever miss me from the movement and couldn't find me nowhere, come on over to the graveyard, and I'll be buried there!"

The next time I saw Mrs. Hamer was January 21, 1964. It was Freedom Day in Hattiesburg, in southern Mississippi. SNCC would try to have hundreds of black Mississippians register to vote, in a county where not one black person was registered.

I sat in on the strategy session for Freedom Day. There would be a mass meeting that night, a picket line around the courthouse the next day. There would be arrests, undoubtedly. A telegram was sent to Attorney General Robert Kennedy: "Tomorrow morning, hundreds of Hattiesburg's citizens will attempt to register to vote. We request the presence of federal marshals to protect them. We also request that local police interfering with constitutional rights be arrested and prosecuted. Signed, Bob Moses." We all knew there would be no reply.

Ella Baker and John Lewis arrived by train from Atlanta to speak at the church meeting, where a thousand people gathered, singing, "We shall not, we shall not be moved. . . ." The other civil rights groups were represented: Annelle Ponder for Martin Luther King's Southern Christian Leadership Conference, Dave Dennis for the Congress of Racial Equality. A rabbi spoke, part of a delegation of fifty clergymen who would join the picket line.

Ella Baker spoke, going beyond the immediate, as she always did, to fundamentals: "Even if segregation is gone, we will still need to be free, we will still have to see that everyone has a job. Even if we can all vote, but if people are still hungry, we will not be free. . . . Singing alone is not enough. We need schools and learning. . . . Remember, we are not fighting for the freedom of the Negro alone, but for the freedom of the human spirit, a larger freedom that encompasses all mankind."

When the meeting was over we all poured out of the building into the darkness. People were still singing. It was almost midnight. There were cots set up at the Freedom House where we would sleep. Over on a long counter a half-dozen people were lettering the picket signs for the morning.

It was 1:00 in the morning, and some of us didn't feel like sleeping. I was assigned to share a cot with a white SNCC man named Mendy Samstein. We were friends from Atlanta, where he had taught briefly at Morehouse as a young graduate student at the University of Chicago, then left to work with SNCC. We had been together in a strange sit-in that in later years we would laugh about: the two of us and two black friends, sitting in at Leb's, a Jewish delicatessen in downtown Atlanta, on Passover.

But we found someone already snoring on our cot. Two more guys joined us: Oscar Chase, a Yale Law School graduate then with SNCC (in later years to become a law professor at New York University), and Avery Williams, who still had scars on his leg from the cattle prods in Selma. Someone handed us a slip of paper with an address. It was 3:00 A.M. when we hesitantly knocked on the door of the house, which was all dark. The man who came to the door was in his pajamas. He smiled broadly. "Come on in!" He shouted through the darkness, back into his bedroom, "Hey, honey, look who's here!" The lights were on now and his wife came out. "Can I fix something for you fellows?" We said no, and apologized for getting them up. The man waved his hand. "Oh, I was going to get up soon anyway."

The man dragged out a mattress for us. "Here, two of you can sleep on the mattress, one on the couch, and we have a little cot." I awoke at dawn, and in the semidarkness I could see my friends near me, still asleep. I became aware of the sound that had awakened me; at first I had thought it part of a dream, but I still heard it now, a woman's voice, pure and poignant, chanting softly.

At first I thought it came from outside, then I realized it was coming from the bedroom. The man was already gone to work, and his wife was praying, intoning, "Oh, Lord Jesus. Oh, let things go well today, Jesus . . . Oh, make them see, Jesus . . . Show your love today, Jesus . . . Oh, it's been a long time, oh, Jesus . . . Oh, Lord. Oh, Jesus. . . ."

Avery awoke. A radio was turned on with dance music played loud. A light went on in the kitchen. As we dressed I looked through the open doorway into the couple's bedroom and saw there was no mattress on their bed. They had given us theirs.

The woman made breakfast, a feast—eggs and grits and bacon and hot biscuits and coffee. She told us her husband drove down to the Gulf every morning to work on the fishing docks. She was soon to be picked up in a truck and taken off to work as a maid. As we prepared to leave, Avery Williams looked outside: "It's raining!"

When we arrived at the county courthouse, a picket line was already formed. Two lines of policemen came down the street; a police car swung to the curb, a loudspeaker on its roof: "This is the Hattiesburg Police Department. We're asking you to disperse. Clear the sidewalk." John Lewis and I stood across the street in front of Sears Roebuck, on the sidewalk. None of us made a move to leave. About fifty black youngsters arrived to join the picket line.

People prepared to register were lined up on the steps outside the glass door, which was guarded by a sheriff. The Justice Department had secured a court injunction against discrimination by the registrar. That was as far as they would go. The registrar was complying—minimally. Four people were admitted every hour, the rest having to line up on the steps, exposed to the rain. By noon, twelve people had filled out applications.

At 10:00 the drizzle had become a downpour. Jim Forman stood just outside the glass door of the courthouse, shirt collar open under his raincoat, pipe in his right hand, gesticulating with his left hand, black men and women bunched around him. He was calling to the sheriff to ask him to let these people inside the courthouse, out of the rain.

Someone said that Bob Moses had just been taken off to jail, ar-

rested for standing on the sidewalk opposite the courthouse and refusing to move on.

The picket line continued all afternoon. I could see the familiar
form of Mrs. Hamer, moving along with her characteristic limp,
holding a sign, her face wet with the rain and turned upwards,
crying out her song against the sky: "Which Side Are You On?"
After a while I took the picket sign from her and walked the line
while she rested on the steps.

Later, in the summer of 1964, Mrs. Hamer went to the Atlantic
City Democratic Party Convention with other black Mississippians, to demand of the Democratic big-wigs that blacks be represented in what was an all-white Mississippi delegation. She appeared on television to move the nation—if not the Democratic
party—with her indignation: "I'm sick and tired of being sick and
tired!" (She visited me in Boston some time after that, on her way
to an audience with Cardinal Cushing, whom she had been briefed
to address as "Your Eminence"; she told me, laughing, that she was
afraid she would slip and address him as "Your Enemy.")

At 5:00 the picket line at the Hattiesburg courthouse ended. It
was something of a victory—no mass arrests, no beatings.

There was one more piece of news. Oscar Chase had been arrested. His car had bumped a parked truck, doing no damage, but
that didn't matter; he was taken off to jail for "leaving the scene of
an accident."

I slept that night in the Freedom House. In the morning someone came along to say that Oscar Chase had phoned in to headquarters from the jail. He had been beaten the night before, and
wanted to be bonded out. I went with two of the visiting ministers
to get him.

As we entered the jailhouse a few minutes before 8:00 A.M., the
police dogs were growling and barking in their kennels. We turned
over the bond money.

A moment later, Oscar came down the corridor unescorted. A
few moments before, the corridor had been full of policemen, but
now there was not a soul around. Oscar was still wearing his badly
worn corduroy pants, and his old boots, caked with mud. His blue

workshirt was splattered with blood, and under it his T-shirt was very bloody. The right side of his face was swollen. His nose looked as if it were broken. Blood was caked over his eye.

He told us what had happened. They had put a prisoner into his cell who was in a state of great agitation, very upset about the demonstration at the courthouse. He had been a paratrooper in World War II and told Oscar he "would rather kill a nigger lover than a Nazi or a Jap." He pushed a cigarette near Oscar's face and said he would burn his eyes out. Oscar called for the jailer and asked to be removed from the cell. The ex-paratrooper asked if Oscar was "one of them nigger-lovers." The jailer nodded. The next thing Oscar knew he was lying on the floor. He had been unconscious. Now he was being kicked. He was bleeding. The police came and took the ex-paratrooper out of the cell. Oscar made his phone call.

We arranged to take him to one of the two black doctors in town, but first I and two lawyers would show him to the FBI. The four of us waited in the FBI office for the interrogating agent to come out and get the facts about the beating. The two attorneys were impeccably dressed: John Pratt, an attorney with the National Council of Churches, tall, blond, slender, in a dark suit with faint stripes; Robert Lunney, of the Lawyer's Committee on Civil Rights, dark-haired and clean-cut, attired as befit an attorney with a leading Wall Street firm. I did not come up to their standards (my pants had lost their press from the rain the day before), but I was clean-shaven and not too disreputable-looking.

Oscar sat with us, looking just as he did when I saw him come out of his cell, his face swollen, his clothes bloody. The FBI agent came out from the inner office and closed the door behind him. He surveyed the four of us with a quick professional eye and then asked, "Who was it got the beating?"

At 4:00 that afternoon, the Hattiesburg Municipal Court convened to hear the case of Robert Moses, on trial for obstructing traffic by standing on the sidewalk and refusing to move on when ordered by a policeman. We had decided in advance that we would "integrate" the courtroom, although every previous attempt at that had met with arrests. I sat on the "colored" side with about ten other whites, and an equal number of blacks sat on the "white" side. Nine marshals stood against the wall.

The judge entered the chamber and everyone rose. To our surprise, it was a woman, Judge Mildred W. Norris, a gracious lady who smiled and posed for the photographers as she approached the bench, then nodded for everyone to be seated. She smiled pleasantly at the spectators, paused for a moment, then said sweetly, "Will the marshals please segregate the courtroom?"

Everything was quiet. The marshals moved toward us. The judge said, "I will ask you to please move to the side of the courtroom where you belong, or leave. If you do not, you will be held in contempt of court and placed under arrest." None of us moved. The marshals came closer.

As one approached me I raised my hand. He stopped and said, rather uncertainly, "Do you wish to make a statement?" "Yes," I replied. The judge said, "You may make a statement." I got to my feet and said, "Your honor, the Supreme Court of the United States has ruled that segregated seating in a courtroom is unconstitutional. Will you please abide by that ruling?" The courtroom buzzed. The judge hesitated. John Pratt, the movement attorney, asked for a recess of a few minutes, and the judge granted it.

During the recess no one changed seats. The judge reconvened the court, and the room was absolutely silent. She surveyed the situation, glanced at the marshals along the wall, and said, "We here in Mississippi have had our way of life for hundreds of years, and I obey the laws of Mississippi. I have asked that you sit segregated or leave or be placed under arrest. We would have appreciated your complying." She paused. "But since you do not, we will allow you to remain as you are, providing you do not create a disturbance."

We sat there astonished. The trial began: *John Quincy Adams v. Robert Moses* (Adams was the arresting officer, and the case came to be called *Adams v. Moses*). Three policemen took the stand and testified that Moses had obstructed pedestrian traffic by standing on the sidewalk. Cross-examined, John Quincy Adams admitted that no other pedestrians had complained about the sidewalk being obstructed and that he had not seen anyone who did not have free access.

The courtroom was very hot and the judge began fanning herself with a cardboard sign near her. It was one of the exhibits, a picket sign with large letters: "Freedom Now."

Bob Moses took the stand, to be examined by a bullying prosecutor. He answered in a quiet, even voice, pointing out patiently again and again where the prosecutor had misunderstood his reply, occasionally blinking his eyes under the glare of the lights in the courtroom, but looking steadily, seriously at his questioner.

At the end of the day's testimony, the judge found Moses guilty, sentenced him to a fine of $200 and sixty days in jail, and Patrolman John Quincy Adams took him back to his cell.

(After the movement quieted, Bob Moses went to Tanzania to teach for some years, with another veteran of the Mississippi struggle, Janet Lamott, and their four children were born in Africa; he then returned to study Eastern philosophy at Harvard and to organize new ways of teaching math to poor kids all over the country.)

Moses was out on bail in a few days, and, with SNCC and other civil rights organizations, set about making plans for the big Freedom Summer in Mississippi, with a thousand students set to arrive to help with voter registration and other matters. And for the first time since Reconstruction, a group of Mississippi blacks announced as candidates for Congress. One of them was Mrs. Fannie Lou Hamer of Ruleville.

Roz and I went back to Mississippi for that Freedom Summer. She helped out in the Jackson office. I was one of many teachers in the Freedom Schools, where two thousand black youngsters, meeting in church basements all over Mississippi, had a taste of an extraordinary experiment in democratic education. They were given a chance to both read and write poems and stories, to write and perform dramas and musicals, to role-play confrontations with racism, to argue about the Bill of Rights, to spend a whole morning on the word "skeptical." The Freedom Schools were a momentary glimpse of a whole new way of education, not only for Mississippi, but for the country.

It was a summer of violence. Three civil rights workers, two white, one black, were arrested in the city of Philadelphia, Neshoba County; let out in the night, they were followed and shot to death. Their bodies had not yet been found when a number of us drove up, on a crazy impulse, to the annual Neshoba County Fair. It was, altogether, an eerie experience. At one point we found ourselves a few feet from the sheriff and deputy sheriff who, we were sure, had participated in the disappearance of the three men.

It was a summer after which Mississippi would never be the same, even if some final victory over poverty and racism was still far off, maybe even impossibly far off. It was a summer of great learning for black people, for white people, inside and outside of the movement. So many had their lives changed.

Twenty-five years later, official segregation is finally gone. Unofficial segregation is being challenged on all fronts. But racism, poverty, and police brutality are still the intertwined realities of black life in the United States.

This was clear even in the sixties, when riots exploded in the black ghettos of the country again and again, at the very time civil rights laws were being passed. In the nineties, it was underlined by the police beating of an unarmed, unemployed black man, Rodney King, in Los Angeles, videotaped for the whole country to see. When the black population of the city exploded in anger, it was clear that the deeper cause, beyond police brutality, was pervasive poverty and the nation's neglect.

What the movement accomplished was historic, but soon it came up against obstacles far more formidable than the signs and badges of racial segregation. First, an economic system that, while lavishly rewarding some people and giving enough to others to gain their loyalty, consigns a substantial part of the population to misery, generation after generation. And along with this, a national ideology so historically soaked in racism that nonwhite people inevitably form the largest part of the permanent poor.

Against these obstacles the civil rights movement, courageous as it was, far-sighted as some of its leaders were (both Martin Luther King, Jr., and Malcolm X understood the *depth* of the problem beyond segregation), was unprepared.

What the movement proved, however, is that even if people lack the customary attributes of power—money, political authority, physical force—as did the black people of the Deep South, there is a power that can be created out of pent-up indignation, courage, and the inspiration of a common cause, and that if enough people put their minds and bodies into that cause, they can win. It is a phenomenon recorded again and again in the history of popular movements against injustice all over the world.

There is no sign of such a movement in the early nineties. But the *need* for it is clear, and the ingredients for it are all around, waiting to be put together. There is a new generation of militant black youth, with enormous energy too often misused or wasted but capable of being mobilized if the right time and conditions appear. There are millions of people, white and nonwhite, increasingly impatient with the system's failure to give them, however eager they are to work hard, security in jobs, in housing, in health care, in education.

The movement at least *began* to shake things up. One aspect of national life in particular has been shaken up—culture. People in music, cinema, sports, even while surrounded by racial antagonism, have pioneered in bringing the races together. This cultural change, so at odds with the brooding resentments of the inner city, may well prepare the way for a rainbow coalition that could challenge the political and economic system.

When that might happen is uncertain. *If* that can happen is also uncertain. But not to believe in the possibility of dramatic change is to forget that things *have* changed, not enough, of course, but enough to show what is possible. We have been surprised before in history. We can be surprised again. Indeed, we can *do* the surprising.

The reward for participating in a movement for social justice is not the prospect of future victory. It is the exhilaration of standing together with other people, taking risks together, enjoying small triumphs and enduring disheartening setbacks—together.

These years, when I attend reunions of SNCC people, and we sing and talk, everyone says, in various ways, the same thing: how awful they were, those days in the South, in the movement, and how they were the greatest days of our lives.

PART TWO

War

A Veteran
against War

I joined the Army Air Corps in early 1943—I was twenty years old—eager to get into combat against the Nazis. I could have remained in the Brooklyn Navy Yard, where I had been working for three years, and where our building of battleships and landing ships kept us exempt from military service. But I could not bear to stay out of a war against fascism. I saw the war as a noble crusade against racial superiority, militarism, fanatic nationalism, expansionism.

Without my parents' knowledge (they were for the war, but one of my brothers was already overseas with the army and they wanted me home) I signed up with the Air Corps. I passed all the tests for an aviation cadet—I was a basketball player, in good physical shape, lean (skinny, I thought, but the military seemed not to mind), with perfect eyesight, and the written exams were no problem. I then arranged with my local draft board, through a program called "volunteering for induction," to send me a letter of induction into the military. To make absolutely sure, I asked the draft board clerk if I could mail the induction notice myself, and I dropped it in the mailbox just outside the office.

Before officially becoming an aviation cadet, I had to go through the four-month basic training of an infantryman at Jefferson Barracks, Missouri—forced marches with full field packs and equipment, lots of calisthenics, learning to fire pistols, rifles, carbines, submachine guns, and to distinguish the smells of poison gases. Then to an airfield outside Burlington, Vermont, where I learned to fly a Piper Cub (a ridiculous little toy of a plane; I didn't seriously think they wanted me to get into it). Then to Nashville for a whole set of classification exams to decide if I was best fitted to be a pilot, navigator, or bombardier.

I knew I hadn't done well with the Piper Cub—my instructor was a caricature of the nasty, bullying flight instructor whose favorite instruction to me was a snarling "Get your head out of your ass!" (Admittedly, I had almost killed him several times learning to come out of a spin.) I did very well on the math tests for navigator and on the reflex-coordination tests for bombardier, so I wasn't surprised when I was classified as a bombardier but also scheduled to get some navigation training. We were all put on a troop train headed for preflight training in Santa Ana, California.

After Santa Ana I spent six weeks at a gunnery school outside of Las Vegas, learning to strip and reassemble a 50-calibre machine gun blindfolded, shooting skeet to get into the swing of "leading" enemy planes, then flying over the desert firing machine guns at various targets. In the evening after all that (movies didn't capture how *loud* guns were or how bad they smelled, or what damage the recoil did to your shoulder), we relaxed by going into Las Vegas and gambling with our meager pay, enjoying the gentle sounds of dice and the roulette wheel.

Then four months in the desert country of Deming, New Mexico, learning all about the famous hush-hush Norden bombsight— theory and practice. We flew at different altitudes and dropped bombs on little huts set up in the desert. (There were two rectangles on the map we had to avoid—we didn't know why—near the towns of Alamagordo and Los Alamos.) I was good at it, had a low CE (circular error, or number of feet from the target), and graduated from bombing school with the gold bars of a second lieutenant on my shoulders and bombardier's wings pinned on my chest at graduation. I now had my first furlough since my induction, eleven days to spend at home before joining a crew and going overseas. I took the long train ride from El Paso to New York.

The first thing I did after seeing my parents was to call on the girl I had been writing to and hadn't seen for a year and a half. We had lived in the same shabby, lively Brooklyn neighborhood but had never met until sometime in 1942, when a fellow basketball player then in the army wrote to me and asked me to deliver some of his insignia to a girl he liked but was too shy to get in touch with. Her name was Roslyn Shechter. I had found the street and the apartment and the girl and fulfilled my friend's request. She was finishing washing the kitchen floor; her parents were there, and she suggested we go outside.

We took a walk around the block. She had long chestnut-blonde hair and blue eyes and the face of a Russian beauty, and we had lots to talk about. We discovered that we were both readers: I was reading Marx and Engels and Upton Sinclair, she was reading Dostoevsky and Tolstoy. We seemed to share the same outlook on the world, the war, fascism, socialism. We circled the block several times. I decided I was not really betraying my friend in the service; he was not on her mind.

A few weeks later I invited Roz on a moonlight sail organized for the young workers of the Brooklyn Navy Yard. She wore, very gracefully, a cotton dress which her mother had made. I wore, very awkwardly, a blue sport shirt which my mother had sewn together for me, and a mustard-colored sport jacket which we both still remember as slightly repulsive. But it was a star-filled, romantic evening, and when the sail was over after midnight we didn't want to go home, so we went bowling.

I took her home around 4:00 A.M. Her father was waiting, and furious. A twenty-year-old shipyard worker with outrageously radical political views was not his notion of a proper boyfriend for his princess of a daughter.

Roz and I went out on a few more dates, but I seemed to be just one of a number of fellows in her life. So when I went off into the

Army Air Corps in early 1943 we were not really "boyfriend and girlfriend." But I was lonely in basic training, and I found myself thinking about Roz. I wrote to her, a long letter about what it was like in the military. Waiting for her reply, I went day after day to mail call, always a long time before they got to Z. But nothing came. Months passed and I decided, with a sinking heart, that she did not want to encourage any expectations on my part. There were those other guys, and I had terrible thoughts about what was going on while I was far away. But I wrote a second letter. A reply came quickly. She had not received my first letter. (Had her parents intercepted it? We never found out.)

We began writing more and more frequently. The letters became more intimate. She sent me a photo of herself, looking very lovely, which I kept near my bunk. I could now claim, without saying it, that I had a girlfriend.

We had never mentioned marriage in our sixteen-month correspondence, but when I came home on that eleven-day furlough after getting my wings, sometime during our first evening together alone, a little dizzy with passion, we decided to get married. Four days later, I in uniform, Roz in a skirt and sweater, our hastily assembled (and somewhat bewildered) parents and brothers and sisters in attendance, we were married in the home of a red-headed rabbi, his nine kids looking on from the stairway. A week of "honeymoon" in a cheap hotel in Manhattan, and I left for Rapid City, South Dakota, to meet my air crew.

The Allied invasion of Europe—D-day—was already under way. I was so anxious to get into combat that twice in the next months I traded places with other bombardiers to get on the short list for overseas. Roz agreed—she was as antifascist as I. (But years later she asked, Were we crazy?)

In Rapid City, the crew had several weeks learning to work together, flying the plane we would use in combat, the B-17 Flying Fortress—four engines, with a swiveling ball turret underneath, another gun turret above, a tail gunner, a radio man, an engineer, and, sticking out in front of and below the pilot and co-pilot, the scarily vulnerable plexiglass nose that I shared with the navigator and which housed my bombsight, along with four 50-calibre machine guns.

Roz arrived by train in Rapid City and this was our real honeymoon, in the cold, clean air of the South Dakota winter, in sight of Mount Rushmore, with Deadwood and the Black Hills nearby. Three other crew members had wives who came for what might be the last chance together, and we all became very close. When we flew night flights the women would get together in one of the cabins and cook spaghetti. Finished with our "bombing" we would fly back to base and on the way buzz the cabin to let them know we'd be there soon for a midnight meal.

The women went back home, and our crew sailed on the Queen Mary to England, sixteen thousand troops packed into the luxury liner. We were told that the ship could outrun German submarines, but we didn't believe it.

The officers on board were all given supervisory jobs, and mine was to "keep order" in the huge mess hall where the troops ate twice a day, in four shifts. The four thousand black soldiers on board, who slept in the depths of the ship near the engine room, ate last.

(It seems absurd—but is so typical of whites in this country—that I hadn't *noticed* the absence of blacks in basic training at Jefferson Barracks until one day I took a long walk through the base and found myself in an all-black environment. What I remember most vividly is a squad of black soldiers taking a break on the grass near me, singing "Ain't Gonna Study War No More!" I was startled. I had never heard white troops sing that.)

On the fifth day at sea, there was a mix-up, and the last shift was sent into the mess hall before the previous one was finished eating— four thousand black men pouring into the hall, filling in wherever other men had finished and left. It was now, accidentally, a racially integrated dining hall.

"Lieutenant!" A white sergeant, sitting next to a black man, was calling to me. "Get him out of here until I finish." This angered me, and for the first time in my military career I pulled rank. I shook my head. "If you don't want to finish your food, you can leave.

What the hell is this war all about, sergeant?" It was a long way to the next meal, and the sergeant stayed and ate. I learned something from that little incident, later reinforced in my years in the South: that most racists have something they care about *more* than racial segregation, and the problem is to locate what that is.

On that ocean crossing, the class system of the military was especially evident. Our nine-man crew, who had become good friends—no saluting, no "yessir and nosir"—were separated on board ship. The five enlisted men in the crew ate in the huge mess room, the usual grubby army food. We, the officers, ate in what must have been the first-class dining room of the Queen Mary—linen tablecloths, white-jacketed waiters, magnificent chandeliers, steaks and roasts. It was bizarre, with us sailing through submarine-infested waters on the way to a war.

Landing in England, we were transported to our air base in East Anglia, which bulges eastward toward Holland and Germany. Then it was life in a quonset hut—sleeping bags, cold water, rationed food—and flying what turned out to be the last missions of the war.

Mostly "milk-runs" (no enemy fighters, light flak from the ground)—bombing Berlin, Pilsen, other places in Germany, Hungary, and Czechoslovakia. But the day we flew to Regensburg, the intelligence report was "heavy flak," meaning that as you approached the target the sky was so thick with black exploding shells it seemed impossible to fly through and come out alive. That morning I argued vehemently with another bombardier who claimed *he* was due to fly that mission, but I insisted and won. We were both war-crazed, wanting to rack up more missions, not seeming to understand that the more missions we flew the more likely we were to die.

And there was one mission where the first German jets of the war appeared—frighteningly fast, in three passes taking out three of the twelve planes in our group, then disappearing (those first jets could not stay aloft very long).

The war was about to be over, obviously, in days or weeks, but one morning we were yanked out of our sleep at 1:00 A.M. and told we were going on another bombing mission.

It was not like the movies, with Robert Taylor leaping out of his bed into the cockpit and flying off. Five hours between waking and the take-off at dawn. Hours of briefings—crew briefings, officers' briefings, bombardiers' briefings. Then eating a breakfast with "round eggs" (that meant real eggs, which we got in unlimited quantities the mornings we were going on a mission; on other days we got "square eggs," powdered eggs in pancake form). Then the equipment: electrically heated suit, sheepskin clothes on top of that in case of electrical failure, oxygen mask and throat mike, a flak vest (a heavy leaden monstrosity we didn't bother to wear—too much trouble just to save a life), a flak helmet, heavy and awkward (which we sometimes wore). Check the bombsight, check the guns, check the oxygen system, check the parachutes, check everything.

The briefing officer told us about the mission. We were going to bomb a little town named Royan, near Bordeaux, on the Atlantic coast of France. (After the war I learned that it was a resort town for French vacationers; Picasso swam there.) We looked at one another: France? Our armies had already overrun France, were well into Germany.

The explanation came: there were a few thousand German soldiers holed up near Royan, waiting for the war to end, and we were to take them out. And we would not be carrying in our bomb bay the usual load of twelve five-hundred-pound demolition bombs (it was the bombardier's job, once in enemy territory, to crawl back to the bomb bay and "arm" the bombs, that is, remove the cotter pins so that they became live). Instead, each bomb bay would carry something new, thirty one-hundred-pound canisters of "jellied gasoline"—sticky fire. They didn't use the word, and I only realized long after the war that this was an early use of *napalm*.

So, we destroyed the German forces (twelve hundred Flying Fortresses bombing several thousand German soldiers!)—and also the French population of Royan. After the war, I read a dispatch by the *New York Times* correspondent in the area: "About 350 civilians, dazed or bruised . . . crawled from the ruins and said the air attacks had been 'such hell as we never believed possible.' ' "

At our bombing altitudes—twenty-five or thirty thousand feet—we saw no people, heard no screams, saw no blood, no torn limbs. I remember only seeing the canisters light up like matches flaring one by one on the ground below. Up there in the sky, I was just "doing my job"—the explanation throughout history of warriors committing atrocities.

The war was over in three weeks. I heard no one question that raid on Royan, why it was necessary. I didn't. It would not have entered my mind to stand up in the briefing room that morning and ask, Why are we killing more people when the war is about to end?

I flew three more missions in the last week of the war—but not to drop bombs. Our cargo was packages of food, which we were to drop on Amsterdam and Rotterdam because the Germans had blown up the dikes, the land was flooded, and people were starving. We flew at three hundred feet, barely three times the wingspan of our plane, with some tension because the Germans had threatened to fire on food-delivering planes and at that altitude we were easy targets.

But it all went beautifully, and as we flew over the city we could see the streets, the roofs, crowded with people waving to us. As we turned away from Amsterdam on our last trip, one of the guys in the crew called over the interphone, "Look down there." On a field just outside the city, there were thousands and thousands of tulips, forming huge letters: "THANK YOU."

There was only one point during the war when a few doubts crept into my mind about the absolute rightness of what we were doing. I'd made friends with a gunner on another crew. We had something in common in that literary wasteland of an air base: we were both readers, and we were both interested in politics. At a certain point he startled me by saying, "You know, this is not a war against fascism. It's a war for empire. England, the United States, the Soviet Union—they are all corrupt states, not morally concerned about Hitlerism, just wanting to run the world themselves. It's an imperialist war."

"Then why are you here?" I asked.

"To talk to guys like you."

I was astonished and deeply impressed that he would be risking his life flying these missions, all to wage his own political warfare inside the military, to persuade others of his point of view. Two weeks after that conversation his plane did not return from a mission. It was shot down and his whole crew killed.

At the time I wasn't convinced by what he said, but I was troubled by it and never forgot it. I didn't realize myself to what extent my mind was changing during the war, but when it was over and I was putting my stuff together, I collected some photos, old navigation logs, and some other mementos, my Air Medal and ribbons with two battle stars, put them into a folder and without thinking wrote on the folder, "Never again."

After victory in Europe, V-E Day, my crew flew back across the Atlantic in our battered B-17 ("Belle of the Brawl"). We had a thirty-day leave before going to the Pacific to take up bombing again, this time on Japan. Roz and I were heading toward a bus to take us into the country to have some time alone before my leave was over. We passed a newsstand around which people were gathered, evidently excited. A fresh pile of papers had just been delivered, and there was this huge headline: ATOMIC BOMB DROPPED ON JAPANESE CITY OF HIROSHIMA. WAR'S END EXPECTED.

I remember our reaction exactly. We were simply happy. We weren't sure what an atomic bomb was, but it looked like just a bigger bomb than what we had been using all along. Now I wouldn't have to go the Pacific and the war would be over—total victory over fascism—and I would be coming home for good.

It was John Hersey's postwar report, *Hiroshima*, that first made me aware of the horrors we visited on that city, made me see what we had done to a city of civilians, to old people and to schoolchildren, made me see the Japanese as human beings, not simply a nation of ferocious, cruel warriors. It led me to match the infamous "death march" on Bataan, that Japanese atrocity, with another kind of death march in Hiroshima, this time *our* atrocity, when dazed, burnt civilians, their flesh hanging, their eyeballs out of their sockets, their limbs torn from their bodies, walked in a stupor through the eerie remains of their flattened city under a drizzle of radioactive vapor.

While I was a fellow at the Harvard Center for East Asian Studies in the fall of 1960 (on temporary leave from Spelman), I did some research on the dropping of the atomic bombs, and published an article called "A Mess of Death and Documents." The most powerful reason given for the bombings of Hiroshima and Nagasaki was that they saved the lives of those who would have died in an invasion of Japan. But the official report of the Strategic Bombing Survey, which interrogated seven hundred Japanese officials right after the war, concluded that the Japanese were on the verge of surrender and would "certainly" have ended the war by December of 1945 even if the bombs had not been dropped on Hiroshima and Nagasaki, and even without an invasion of Japan. Furthermore, the United States, having broken the Japanese code, *knew* the Japanese were on the verge of surrender.

Then why was it done? The research of an American scholar, Gar Alperowitz, pointed to a political motive: to beat the Russians to the punch in defeating Japan, and to demonstrate to them our strength, because they were about to enter the Pacific war.

My experience with Royan suggested additional reasons: the powerful momentum of a military machine which has been built up and is bursting with energy; the disinclination to "waste" a project into which huge amounts of time and money and talent have been expended; the desire to demonstrate a new weapon; the cold disregard for human life which develops in the course of a war; the acceptance of any means, however horrible, once you have entered a war with a belief in the total nobility of your cause.

In August of 1966, Roz and I traveled to Japan at the invitation of a Japanese peace group, to join people from various parts of the world to commemorate the dropping of the bomb and to dedicate ourselves to the elimination of nuclear weapons. We all met in Hiroshima, rebuilt now except for a few things deliberately left standing to remind people of what had happened.

One day we were invited to a "House of Friendship," a kind of community center for survivors of the bomb. We were expected to say a few words of greeting to the people there, and when it was my turn I started to say something, then looked at the men and women sitting on the floor, their faces turned to me, some without legs, others without arms, some with sockets for eyes, or with horrible burns on their faces and bodies. My mind flashed back to my work as a bombardier and I choked up, could not speak.

The following year, Roz and I, driving from Paris to the Atlantic coast, visited the rebuilt town of Royan, spoke to survivors of the wartime bombing, rummaged through documents. We found an additional motive for that senseless slaughter—the need of both the French and the American military for one more victory before the war ended.

Hiroshima and Royan were crucial in my gradual rethinking of what I had once accepted without question—the absolute morality of the war against fascism. Sometime in the sixties, I read with fascination Joseph Heller's *Catch-22*, with its jabs of black humor poking holes in the self-righteous arrogance of the "good guys" fighting against Hitler. Heller's mad but wise antihero, the bombardier Yossarian, warns a fellow flier who talks about "the enemy" that "the enemy is whoever wants to get you killed, whichever side they're on." I knew by this time that we had again and again bombed people on "our side"—not just the French of Royan, but the Czechs of Pilsen and the Chinese of Hankow and Formosa. By the early seventies, when I wrote a book called *Postwar America*, I entitled the chapter on World War II, with deliberate irony, "The Best of Wars."

There is no war of modern times which has been accepted more universally as just. The fascist enemy was so totally evil as to forbid any questioning. They were undoubtedly the "bad guys" and we were the "good guys," and once that decision was made there seemed no need to *think* about what we were doing. But I had become aware, both from the rethinking of my war experiences and my reading of history, of how the environment of war begins to make one side indistinguishable from the other.

That went way back to the Greeks, to the Peloponnesian War as described by Thucydides in the fifth century before Christ. Athens, "the cradle of democracy," the haven of magnificent art and literature, was the "good guy." Sparta, totalitarian, grim, was the "bad guy." But as the war progressed, the Athenians committed more and more atrocities—indiscriminate massacre, enslavement of women and children.

In World War II, we—the United States, France, England, the "civilized world"—had declared our horror at the new phenomenon of modern aerial warfare, the indiscriminate bombing of the civilian populations of cities. The Japanese bombing of Shanghai, the Italian bombing of unarmed Africans in Ethiopia, bombs dropped during the Spanish Civil War on Madrid, the German bombings of Coventry and Rotterdam. Of course, what do you expect of fascists!

And then we were in the war and doing the same thing, except on a much larger scale. Royan was a minor event. The bombing of Dresden by British and American planes (which Kurt Vonnegut deals with in his own odd way in his unforgettable *Slaughterhouse Five*) killed at least thirty-five thousand, perhaps a hundred thousand, people. Incendiary bombs sucked the oxygen out of the city, bringing hurricane-like winds which sent the flames racing through the streets in that phenomenon called a firestorm.

The bombing of the working-class districts of German cities—the death toll perhaps half a million—was a deliberate policy of Winston Churchill and his advisers, with the agreement of the American high command, to break the morale of the German nation.

The more I read, the more I thought about World War II, the more I became convinced that the atmosphere of war brutalizes everyone involved, begets a fanaticism in which the original moral factor (which certainly existed in World War II—opposition to a ruthless tyranny, to brutal aggression) is buried at the bottom of a heap of atrocities committed by all sides.

By the 1960s, my old belief in a "just war" was falling apart. I was concluding that while there are certainly vicious enemies of liberty and human rights in the world, war itself is the most vicious of enemies. And that while some societies can rightly claim to be more liberal, more democratic, more humane than others, the difference is not great enough to justify the massive, indiscriminate slaughter of modern warfare.

Should not the real motivations of governments be scrutinized? They always claim to be fighting for democracy, for liberty, against aggression, to end all wars—but is that not a handy way to mobilize a population to support war, indeed, absolutely necessary because people do not *instinctively* want to fight? I cherished the lines of e.e. cummings:

> i sing of Olaf, glad and big
> whose warmest heart recoiled at war:
> a conscientious object-or

The evidence was powerful: the Allied powers—the United States, England, the Soviet Union—had not gone to war out of compassion for the victims of fascism. The United States and its allies did not make war on Japan when Japan was slaughtering the Chinese in Nanking, did not make war on Franco when he was destroying democracy in Spain, did not make war on Hitler when he was sending Jews and dissidents to concentration camps, did not even take steps *during* the war to save Jews from certain death. They went to war when their national power was threatened.

The hands of Hitler were filthy, but those of the United States were not clean. Our government had accepted, was still accepting, the subordination of black people in what we claimed was a democratic society. Our government threw Japanese families into concentration camps on the racist supposition that anyone Japanese—even if born in this country—could not be allowed to remain free.

True, fascism was not to be tolerated by decent people. But neither was racism or colonialism or slave labor camps—one or another of which was a characteristic of all of the Allied powers. And granted, fascism was *worse*, admitting of no opening for change. But was *war* the answer? Was the only way to deal with fascism to engage in a bloodbath which left forty million people dead?

War may be undertaken for what appears a good cause, against violence, against cruelty, but war itself multiplies the violence, multiplies the cruelty.

I had been an eager bombardier in the war, caught up in a fanaticism which let me participate unquestioningly in atrocious acts. After the war I slowly came to question whether war, however noble "the cause," solves anything, given the warping of moral sensibility, of rational thought, that always accompanies it.

Contemplating the world at the end of the war: Hitler and Mussolini were gone, Japan was defeated, but was militarism gone, or racism, or dictatorship, or hysterical nationalism? Were not the main victors—the United States and the Soviet Union—now building nuclear arsenals that threatened a war which would make Hitler's holocaust look puny?

Nonviolence, pacifism, had an air of a fairy tale—soft, silly, romantic, unrealistic. And yet, by the seventies and eighties there was no question addressed to me by my students that gave me more trouble than, Okay, war is bad, but what would you *do* about fascism? I could not, in honesty, pretend that I had a clear answer, but I felt sure that the answer could not be the slaughter of war.

I was intrigued, after my experience with the civil rights movement in the South, by the phrase that King used, that SNCC used: nonviolent direct action. Not simply passive nonviolence, certainly not surrender or acceptance or appeasement, but action, resistance, engagement, with the determination to keep violence to a minimum. To ask for solutions totally free of violence *was* unrealistic; even the nonviolent marches and protests in the South, the picket lines and sit-down strikes of the labor movement, had resulted in violence.

As I write this in 1993, the world faces starving children in Somalia, brutal ethnic warfare in Bosnia. Passivity is intolerable, yet military action would probably make things worse. The situation is not dissimilar to World War II: some form of *action* is necessary to defend the victims of violence, to relieve suffering, to create safe havens for threatened people. The action should be focused, controlled, intervening between victims and the evil they face but without creating more victims. And in the meantime, we must look for negotiated solutions, even at the expense of national pride, must consider human life more important than boundary lines, must buy time for the achievement of justice without war.

I see this as the central issue of our time: how to find a substitute for war in human ingenuity, imagination, courage, sacrifice, patience.

Yes, patience. I recall a Bertolt Brecht fable. A man living alone answers a knock at the door. There stands Tyranny, armed and powerful, who asks, "Will you submit?" The man does not reply. He steps aside. Tyranny enters and takes over. The man serves him for years. Then Tyranny mysteriously becomes sick from food poisoning. He dies. The man opens the door, gets rid of the body, comes back to the house, closes the door behind him, and says, firmly, "No."

I thought of that story in 1989, when the apparently all-powerful regimes of the Soviet Union and Eastern Europe collapsed in the face of mass protests and demonstrations. If the United States had become impatient somewhere along the line (that almost happened in the Cuban missile crisis of 1962), we might have had nuclear war. I thought of how the power of tyranny is overestimated (not in the short run, but in the long run), and how it can be overcome by the unity, the determination, of apparently powerless people, as I saw happen in the South.

World War II is over. It cannot be replayed. Everything in history, once it has happened, looks as if it *had* to happen exactly that way. We can't imagine any other. But I am convinced of the uncertainty of history, of the possibility of surprise, of the importance of human action in changing what looks unchangeable.

War is not inevitable, however persistent it is, however long a history it has in human affairs. It does not come out of some instinctive human need. It is manufactured by political leaders, who then must make a tremendous effort—by enticement, by propaganda, by coercion—to mobilize a normally reluctant population to go to war. In 1917, the United States government had to send 75,000 lecturers around the country to give 750,000 lectures reaching millions of people, to persuade them that it was right to go to war. For those unpersuaded, there was prison for draft dodgers, prison for people who dared speak against the war.

After the First World War, in which ten million men died on the battlefield for reasons which no one, afterward, could explain, there was a general public horror of war itself. World War II made war acceptable again; it then became the basis for justifying every war that followed it.

For me, my growing abhorrence of war, my rethinking of the justness of even "the best of wars," led me to oppose, from the start, the American war in Vietnam.

"Sometimes to Be Silent Is to Lie": Vietnam

I was witness in the summer of 1964 to a dramatic encounter between the black Southern movement and the war in Vietnam. In
early August, many of us in the movement drove from Jackson,
Mississippi, into Neshoba County to attend the memorial service
for James Chaney, Mickey Schwerner, and Andrew Goodman.
Their bodies, horribly beaten with chains and then riddled with
bullets, had been found about five weeks after they had disappeared
from sight near the town of Philadelphia.

The memorial service took place over a pile of rubble, all that was
left of the Mount Zion Baptist Church, whose burning the three
young men had gone to investigate. It was a quiet, sunny glen, and
our thoughts were turned to Mrs. Chaney, clad in black, mourning
her teenage son.

Bob Moses spoke at the service, and we could see that his usual
calm was missing. He held up that morning's newspaper from Jackson, and read the headline: "President Johnson Says 'Shoot to Kill'
in the Gulf of Tonkin."

Bob spoke with a bitterness we were not accustomed to seeing in him. The government of the United States, he said, was willing to send armed forces halfway around the world for a cause which was incomprehensible, but it was unwilling to send marshals into Mississippi, though asked again and again, to protect civil rights workers from inevitable violence. And now three of them were dead.

The Tonkin incident—the supposed attack on American destroyers by North Vietnamese torpedo boats near the coast of Vietnam—became the excuse for the swift American escalation of the colonial war that the French had lost in 1954 and that the United States had taken over.

The president, the secretary of state, and the secretary of defense were lying to the American public—there was no evidence of any attack, and the American destroyers were not on "routine patrol" but on spying missions. However, Congress and all the major newspapers and television networks accepted the story without question. Congress immediately passed the Tonkin Gulf Resolution, giving President Johnson a blank check for massive intervention in Vietnam.

That fall, preparing to teach at Boston University, I felt immediately that military involvement in Indochina would be disastrous—for the people there, and for us in the United States.

As a schoolboy I had been taught to be proud of our nation's march across the continent—it was always labeled "Westward Expansion." *Expansion*—it seemed almost biological. We just *grew*. The map that showed it was bright and multicolored: green for the Florida Purchase, blue for the Louisiana Purchase, red for the Mexican Cession. All purchases and cessions! So benign.

A little study of history was instructive. To make the country ours, before and after the American Revolution, we had to displace or annihilate the indigenous people who had lived here for thousands of years. We had expanded by using deception and force, by military forays into Florida to persuade Spain to "sell" that to us (no money changed hands), by invading Mexico and taking almost half its land.

Later, the United States embarked on building an overseas empire, coming on the world scene later than the imperial powers of

Europe, but making up quickly for lost time. We used military force to establish American power in Cuba and Puerto Rico, in Haiti and the Dominican Republic, in Central America, in Hawaii and the Philippines.

Knowing this historical background, one had to become somewhat suspicious of our government's motives in Vietnam.

Thus, when our leaders announced in the summer of 1964 that we had been attacked in the Gulf of Tonkin, I didn't really know what had happened, but some facts were plain. Our destroyers were far from home, indeed in the waters of Vietnam. We had been giving military aid to the French army in Indochina and then to our client government in Saigon for years, so we were hardly innocents. We were the greatest naval power in the world, and North Vietnam had a ridiculously small naval force, so we could not claim to be helpless victims of Asian bullies. Secretary of State Rusk told reporters that he could not explain why this tiny country would challenge the mighty U.S. fleet except that "their processes of logic are very different."

History can come in handy. If you were born yesterday, with no knowledge of the past, you might easily accept whatever the government tells you. But knowing a bit of history—while it would not absolutely prove the government was lying in a given instance—might make you skeptical, lead you to ask questions, make it more likely that you would find out the truth.

I knew how often our government (like other governments) had invented excuses to go to war, found handy "incidents." Our history was full of Tonkins:

In the Mexican War, a skirmish between Mexican and American troops on the Texas-Mexico border led President Polk to state that "American blood has been shed on American soil," and to ask Congress for war. Actually, the encounter took place in disputed territory, and Polk's diary shows that he wanted an excuse for war so the United States could take from Mexico what the United States coveted, California and the whole Southwest.

The expulsion of Spain from Cuba (a worthwhile venture) so that the U.S. could take control of Cuba (an unworthy venture) was preceded by a dubious story, never proven, that the Spaniards had exploded the U.S. battleship *Maine* in Havana harbor.

Our seizure of the Philippines (from the Filipinos) was preceded by a manufactured "incident" between Filipino and U.S. troops.

The German sinking of the passenger ship *Lusitania* in World War I was one of the instances of "ruthless" submarine warfare given as a reason to enter that war; years afterward, it was disclosed that the *Lusitania* was not an innocent vessel but a munitions ship whose papers had been doctored.

And now Tonkin. It was later revealed that the destroyer *Maddox* was not on "routine patrol" but was part of a secret intelligence operation against North Vietnam, and that the United States was looking for an excuse to come into the war full-scale.

The Gulf of Tonkin affair was followed by a swift escalation of military force—full-scale bombing, hundreds of thousands of American troops. Reasons were given: the United States was doing all this to defend the right of the South Vietnamese to self-determination, to stop the spread of Soviet Communism, to promote freedom and democracy.

The history of U.S. foreign policy in the twenty years since World War II suggested that these claims were not to be believed. Self-determination? The United States did not respect the self-determination of Iran when the CIA in 1953 engineered a coup to restore the Shah to his throne and thus protect the oil interests of American corporations. Nor did it respect the self-determination of Guatemala when it organized an invasion in 1954 to overthrow a democratically elected government which threatened the interests of the United Fruit Company.

As for promoting freedom and democracy, it was a ludicrous claim considering U.S. support of dictatorships all over the world. Brutal tyrants were tolerable just so long as they were not Communist. Batista in Cuba, Somoza in Nicaragua, Trujillo in the Dominican Republic, Duvalier in Haiti, Marcos in the Philippines— the list of bloody military juntas kept in power by the United States was long.

It was clear that the Soviet Union had created a satellite empire in Eastern Europe, and that the United States did not want to see Communist governments established elsewhere in the world. But it was also clear that *any* government, even if not Communist (Iran and Guatemala, as examples), that defied U.S. business interests or U.S. political power became a target for overthrow.

As for Vietnam, the United States could hardly claim it wanted the Vietnamese to run their own country when it had done everything in its power to help the French establish control over its former colony. It could hardly claim a concern for democracy when the government in South Vietnam, in Saigon, rejected elections (on U.S. orders) and violently suppressed all opposition, whether Communist, or liberal, or Buddhist. (Buddhist monks were setting themselves afire in public squares in Saigon to attract the attention of the world to the tyranny there.)

And now, with no moral claim on any count, the United States was bombing and invading villages in Vietnam, killing large numbers of civilians, destroying a green and fertile land.

I did not have any illusions about the Communist government of North Vietnam, or about a future Communist society in all of Vietnam. I did not expect either to be free or democratic, although they might provide land, medical care, and education more equitably to the poor. But whatever regime Communists might set up in Vietnam, I knew that our invasion and bombing, directed against the population at large, was wrong. I therefore had no hesitation about plunging early into the small movement against the war.

In fact, Americans have a long history of protesting against wars into which their government tries to entice them or force them under threat of prison. The early colonists refused to be conscripted for the British wars with the French, and dissidents in the Revolutionary War resented the rich and powerful leaders of the Revolution as much as they distrusted the British. In the Mexican war, soldiers deserted in great numbers, seven regiments walking away from General Winfield Scott as he prepared for the march into Mexico City. During World War I, the government had to put on trial and imprison thousands of people to suppress their opposition.

The movement against the war in Vietnam started with isolated actions in 1965. Black civil rights activists in the South were among the first to resist the draft. SNCC's Bob Moses joined historian Staughton Lynd and veteran pacifist Dave Dellinger to march in Washington against the war, and *Life Magazine* had a dramatic photo of the three of them walking abreast, being splattered with red paint by angry super-patriots.

In the spring of 1965 I spoke at what was to be the first of many antiwar rallies on the Boston Common. It was a discouragingly small crowd—perhaps a hundred people. I was on the platform with Herbert Marcuse, the German philosopher and radical who would become one of the intellectual heroes of the sixties for the New Left in Europe and the United States.

A year later, in the summer of 1966, with the escalation still going on, with the bombing more ferocious than ever, an invitation came from a Japanese group opposing U.S. intervention in Vietnam. I and Ralph Featherstone, a black SNCC worker I knew from Mississippi, were asked to do a two-week lecture circuit in Japan.

Our hosts, a group called Beheiren, were young intellectuals of the Japanese New Left—novelists, journalists, filmmakers, poets, philosophers, housewives. Their chairman was Oda Makoto, a famous writer, big, tousle-haired, with unpressed coat and trousers, who had studied Greek and Latin, spoke English well, seemed to have an encyclopedic knowledge of world politics, and never wore a tie no matter what the occasion (determined, it seemed, to break the stereotype of the well-dressed, formal Japanese).

Oda and the others were amazing organizers. In fourteen days we spoke at fourteen different universities in nine cities, plus tea gatherings, beer sessions, and press conferences. We found the Japanese virtually unanimous (polls taken by the major Japanese newspapers affirmed this) in their belief that the United States did not belong in Vietnam.

When we took the high-speed train from Tokyo to Kyoto, our host, who met us at the station, was a sweet-faced, mild-mannered philosopher named Tsurumi Shunsuke. He had studied at Harvard and was in his last year there when Pearl Harbor was bombed. Tsurumi was picked up by the police as an enemy alien and put in the Charles Street Jail in Boston.

Tsurumi was interrogated. "Are you loyal to the Japanese government?" He answered, "No." "Are you loyal to the American government." Again his answer was "No." Whereupon they said, "You are an anarchist. You will have to be kept in jail." (Tsurumi was released some time later, when the Red Cross arranged a prisoner exchange.)

It was late at night when he met us at the Kyoto train station. He said, "We thought it would be interesting for each of you to spend the night at a different Buddhist temple." We thanked him. Tsurumi took me to a beautiful temple. The monk, he told me, was a strong antiwar person. In front of the altar was a blown-up photo of a Vietnamese Buddhist monk sitting cross-legged on the street in Saigon, setting himself afire.

In Kyoto a thousand people came to talk about Vietnam. A pediatrician spoke from the audience, and our interpreter whispered to us that this was the famous Dr. Matsuda, the "Dr. Spock of Japan," whose books on child care had sold millions. Matsuda said, "What the United States does not understand is that Communism is *one* of the ways in which underdeveloped countries can become organized. Its reaction to this phenomenon is neurotic. Perhaps the United States needs"—the interpreter hesitated—"a laxative!" There was a short silence, then the interpreter apologized and corrected himself: ". . . a sedative."

We took the night train to Hiroshima, along the inland sea, touched by mountains and beautiful in the predawn. We talked with students at Hiroshima University and to survivors of that day when the city died: a professor whose left eye was missing, a fragile girl who spoke halting English in a voice so soft one had to strain to hear "I was inside my mother when the bomb came."

In the city of Sendai, in northern Honshu island, a thousand students gathered to hear us. Afterward fifty young men and women led us to a nearby park, where we all sat cross-legged on the grass and talked into the wee hours of the morning. They were conscious and ashamed of Japan's history of aggression. Again and again they said, softly but firmly, "You are behaving in Asia as we did."

(After spending two weeks in Japan with Ralph Featherstone, day and night, I didn't see him again. He sent me a wedding announcement, and I heard he was running a bookstore in Washington featuring black literature. Then, about two years after our Japan trip, I had what I can only describe as a mystical experience. I was sitting on a bus in Boston, and several seats in front of me was a black man. I could only see the back of his head and his neck, but I could have sworn it was Ralph Featherstone. Was it possible that he was in Boston? I walked over, sat down next to him, and turned to look. It was not Featherstone at all, but a man I did not know. He was reading a newspaper. I looked at the headline: "Civil Rights Workers Killed in Bomb Blast." And there was a photo of Ralph Featherstone. He had been riding with a friend in an auto on the way to the trial of a SNCC worker in Maryland when a bomb, its origin still unknown today, exploded.)

After my trip to Japan I continued to speak against the war all over the country: teach-ins, rallies, debates. I was becoming frustrated by the fact that no major public figure, no leading periodical, no published book, however critical of the war, dared to say what seemed so clear to me—that the United States must simply *get out* of Vietnam as quickly as possible, to save American lives, to save Vietnamese lives. Again and again, these cautious critics of the war would say, The war is wrong, but of course we can't simply withdraw.

I wrote, as quickly as I could, a little book of a hundred and twenty-five pages, which Beacon Press published in early 1967, called *Vietnam: The Logic of Withdrawal.* I said in the book, "To wait until all of the sensitive and stubborn elements are fitted together in that intricate mechanism of negotiation—the NLF, its sympathizers and advisers in Hanoi, the split personalities of the Johnson administration, plus its client government in Saigon—is to consign thousands more each month to injury or death. . . . The sanity of unilateral withdrawal is that it makes the end of the war independent of anyone's consent but our own. It is clean-cut, it is swift, it is right."

Various people had said to me, Yes, I agree. But it's not politically feasible—how can the president explain to the American people the sudden change in policy?

I decided therefore to end my book with a speech which I wrote for Lyndon Johnson, making use of all his powers of rhetoric, his homespun stories, having him quote "a letter" he received from his old elementary school teacher, another "letter" from a marine, and explain to the American people how both realism and concern for human life required a change in policy. And so, "I have given orders to General Westmoreland . . . to halt offensive operations and to begin the orderly withdrawal of our armed forces from that country."

The speech ended, "The dream I have always had since I was a boy in Texas, I still have—and I want to fulfill it for America. We are about to embark on a venture far more glorious, far more bold, requiring far more courage—than war. Our aim is to build a society which will set an example for the rest of mankind. . . . My fellow Americans, good night and sleep well. We are no longer at war in Vietnam."

The book went quickly through eight printings. Two Beacon Press employees traveled with carloads of the book to sell it at antiwar rallies. A businessman bought over six hundred copies and sent them to every congressman, every senator. Senator Ernest Gruening of Alaska (only he and Senator Wayne Morse of Oregon had voted against the Tonkin Gulf Resolution) inserted part of the book in the Congressional Record.

In Santa Barbara, California, a group of citizens took a full-page ad in the local paper, reprinted excerpts from the book, and called for a peace procession.

The *Cleveland Plain Dealer* ran simultaneous articles by Congressman Mendel Rivers of South Carolina, urging escalation of the war; by Senator William Fulbright of Arkansas, calling for de-escalation and negotiations; and by me, arguing for immediate withdrawal. They polled their readers to see which of the three positions they favored: 9,162 responded, and 63 percent favored immediate withdrawal; the rest split equally between the Fulbright and Rivers positions.

The same articles were reprinted in the Charleston, West Virginia *Gazette-Mail*, and 80 percent of readers polled favored immediate withdrawal.

A columnist for the *Plain Dealer* wrote, "Howard Zinn, a professor of government at Boston University, who served as a bombardier in World War II, has written a speech for Lyndon Johnson which, if he delivered it, would make the President one of the great men of history, in my opinion."

All of this was enormously encouraging. Despite the attempts of the government to play down the protests against the war, and to suppress them, it seemed clear there was a large section of the American public open to the idea of withdrawal from Vietnam. This meant there was a point to our speaking, writing, protesting, and we must continue.

President Johnson never delivered that speech, or one like it. He did pull out of the 1968 presidential race, and began negotiations in Paris with the North Vietnamese. But the negotiations then went on for four years while the bombing and strafing and search-and-destroy missions continued and the body bags of twenty thousand more American soldiers were sent home to their families.

Desertions from the military multiplied. About a year after my trip to Japan I was awakened in the middle of the night by a phone call. A Japanese speaking English was on the other end. He told me his name. It was one of my Beheiren friends. "Howard, can you come to Tokyo? There are some Americans here you would be interested in meeting."

I knew what he meant. Beheiren had been helping American servicemen based in Japan who wanted to desert, hiding them, getting them out of the country. They wanted someone to interview a few men before they disappeared.

"When would I have to come?" I asked.

"Tomorrow." I couldn't pick up and travel to Tokyo the next day, but I promised I would find another person to do it. I had someone in mind: Ernest Young, a professor of Asian history at Dartmouth. Roz and I had become close friends with Ernie and his wife Marilyn when they were graduate students in Asian studies at Harvard and I was a Fellow there. Ernie was deeply opposed to the war; he had worked in the American Embassy in Tokyo at one time as an aide to Ambassador Reischauer; he spoke Japanese.

Early that morning, a few hours after the call from Tokyo, I phoned Ernie in Hanover, New Hampshire. That afternoon he arrived at our house in Boston, suitcase in hand, and I drove him to the airport. When he got to Tokyo the Beheiren people arranged a clandestine meeting with four sailors who were deserting from the aircraft carrier *Intrepid* (they became known as the Intrepid Four). Ernie talked to them, then Beheiren smuggled them onto a Polish freighter going to Europe. (Years later, when I got my FBI file—at least that part of it they were willing to give me—they had a record of the phone call from Tokyo, so it seems my phone was tapped.)

By early 1968, the war was at its most intense. There were now 525,000 U.S. troops in South Vietnam. The antiwar movement had grown; resistance to the draft was widespread. All over the country young men were turning in their draft cards, and many others were refusing induction.

The horrors inflicted by American firepower were coming home, reported in news dispatches, in the letters of soldiers, on television screens. For the first time in our nation's history, Americans could see close up the effects of war: the torching of peasant villages by U.S. Marines, Vietnamese children frightened, wounded, disfigured by napalm. A friend told me how one day, driving through Boston listening to the latest war news, she thought of the waste of lives, Vietnamese and American, and, overwhelmed by grief and frustration, began to cry and almost lost control of the car.

A student of mine at Boston University named Philip Supina, summoned to a preinduction physical, wrote to his draft board in

Arizona, "I have absolutely no intention to report for that exam or for induction, or to aid in any way the American war effort against the people of Vietnam." Sentenced to four years in prison, Supina quoted the Spanish philosopher Miguel Unamuno, who said during the Spanish Civil War, "Sometimes to be Silent is to Lie."

The Last
Teach-In

The remarkable growth of the antiwar movement can be measured by the size of the rallies on the Boston Common as they grew from year to year after that first poorly attended one in the spring of 1965. Two years later, a rally on the Common brought thousands of people. It was observed by the FBI and is described in an entry in my FBI file.

I got that file under the Freedom of Information Act—several hundred pages, mostly boring, with many blacked-out sections, but reminding me of many forgotten rallies and speeches. The FBI is supposed to investigate criminal activities, but, like the old Soviet secret police, it seems also to take note of gatherings and public statements where the government is criticized.

The FBI file reported: "On October 16, 1967, a public anti-draft protest demonstration took place on the Boston Common . . . with an estimated 4000–5000 individuals, males and females, in attendance. This protest demonstration . . . was observed by Special Agents of the F.B.I. Among the speakers appearing at this demonstration was Professor Howard Zinn. . . . The morning edition of the *Boston Globe* . . . carried an article captioned '67 Burn Draft Cards in Boston—214 Turn in Cards, 5000 at Rally.'"

The FBI report also reproduced some of my speech as reported in the *Globe*: "The 13,000 Americans who died in Vietnam died because they were sent there under the orders of politicians and generals who sacrificed them on behalf of their own ambitions. . . . We owe it to our conscience, to the people of this country, to the principles of American democracy, to declare our independence of this war, to resist it in every way we can, until it comes to an end, until there is peace in Vietnam."

The people assembled on the Common that morning then marched to the historic Arlington Street Church, where they crowded into the ancient pews to listen to William Sloane Coffin, the Yale chaplain, and Michael Ferber, a Harvard graduate student (both would be indicted, with Dr. Benjamin Spock and writers Mitchell Goodman and Marcus Raskin, for conspiring against the draft law). Coffin, whom I had met years before in New Haven, was one of the antiwar movement's most eloquent speakers. Ferber was new to it, but made an extraordinary, passionate, personal statement.

Then the historic church candlestick, placed there over a century before by the antislavery preacher William Ellery Channing, was held up as young men approached it and held their draft cards to the flame.

The scene was being enacted all over the country, with draft cards either burned or collected to be turned in to the Justice Department in Washington. And the following day a huge antiwar rally at the Lincoln Memorial culminated at night with an eerie confrontation at the Pentagon, thousands of protesters facing thousands of National Guardsmen and Army regulars. At one point a former Green Beret, now a protester, speaking through a bullhorn to the soldiers, told why he had turned against the war.

By 1968, antiwar feeling was so widespread that President Johnson had to cancel all his public appearances except those at military bases. He was told by a special group of advisers that he should not send more troops to Vietnam because the country would not stand for it. It was at that point that he announced he would not run for reelection. Both Richard Nixon and Hubert Humphrey, in their campaigns for the presidency that year, had to promise that they would bring the war to an end.

Nixon, elected president, continued the war, and the antiwar movement declared October 15, 1969, a Moratorium Day—asking that everyone stop business as usual and gather in demonstrations throughout the country. Several thousand of us marched from Boston University down Commonwealth Avenue, and it seemed that every few blocks more thousands joined. As we approached the Common we saw marchers converging from all directions. Those of us who were on the speakers' platform could see the Common packed with people—men, women, children—as far as the eye could see, a hundred thousand or more. I could not help thinking of that tiny group of a hundred who had come to that first meeting on the Common.

That day, throughout the nation, in towns and cities that had never seen an antiwar rally, several million people were protesting the war. It was the largest public demonstration in the nation's history.

On Moratorium Day I was racing from one antiwar rally to another, as so many others were, our voices hoarse by the end of the day. At one point I drove past the Newton College of the Sacred Heart, a staid, conservative Catholic school for young women, where early in the war I had been invited by an antiwar nun to speak and had received a polite but definitely cold reception. Now, as I passed, I saw on its entrance gate a huge banner with a painted red fist and the words "STOP THE WAR!"

At Boston University, antiwar activity was intense, with rallies and building occupations and all-night teach-ins. I recall speaking at three in the morning in the university's largest auditorium to an audience struggling to stay awake but determined to show their solidarity. The campus newspaper, under the editorship of the fiery Ray Mungo, had made national news by calling for the impeachment of Lyndon Johnson. We gave sanctuary to a deserting GI, a thousand students and faculty filling the university's chapel for five days and nights, until federal agents kicked and pushed their way through the tightly-massed group early one Sunday morning, smashed down a door, and took the GI into custody. President Nixon, making a gesture toward his campaign promises, began withdrawing troops, but he also launched secret bombings of Cambodia, with which the United States was not at war. In early 1969 and 1970, he extended the ground war to Laos and Cambodia, the two neighbors of Vietnam, in a vain effort to stop the infiltration of North Vietnamese troops into South Vietnam.

The Cambodian invasion provoked nationwide protests, and on the campus of Kent State University, in Ohio, trigger-happy National Guardsmen fired into a crowd of unarmed student demonstrators, killing four of them, crippling another for life. A photo flashed around the world showed an unnamed young woman, her face anguished, bending over the body of one of the dead students.

On television I saw the father of one of the victims, Allison Krause, barely able to control his grief, pointing to the fact that President Nixon had referred to student protesters as "bums." He cried out, "My daughter was not a bum!"

A few years later, when some visiting parents were sitting in on the introductory session of my course "Law and Justice in America," I handed out the syllabus, which included as one of the course topics the shootings at Kent State. At the end of the session, one of the new students came up and introduced herself and her parents. She was Laurie Krause, the sister of Allison. I recognized her father from the television screen and felt a pang of unease that their unspeakable grief was represented so matter-of-factly on a course syllabus. But they seemed to appreciate that the Kent State affair was not forgotten.

The spring of 1970 saw the first general student strike in the history of the United States, students at over four hundred colleges and universities calling off classes to protest the invasion of Cambodia, the Kent State affair, the killing of two black students at Jackson State College in Mississippi, and the continuation of the war.

That June I was the invited commencement speaker at Queens College in New York, and several thousand graduates and parents crowded Madison Square Garden for the ceremony. My comments on the war and on the U.S. government brought some of the parents to their feet with shouts of anger, but when I finished the graduates rose from their seats and applauded for a long time.

Even more striking was that high school students all over the country, stimulated by the civil rights movement and the antiwar movement, were demanding more democracy, more of a voice in decisions affecting them. In my town of Newton, Massachusetts, that June of 1970, students at the local high school won the right to choose their own commencement speaker. They invited me.

By this time I had spoken against the war at hundreds of situations around the country—teach-ins, rallies, debates. But nowhere did an invitation to speak bring such a violent reaction as did the one from Newton North High School. I learned something from this: that the high school years must be the most important years in shaping the social consciousness of young people, because at no other level do parents and school officials become more hysterical at the possibility that the students will be exposed to ideas which challenge the authority of government, of school administrations, of parents.

The local veterans' organizations in Newton immediately called for a boycott of the commencement. The mayor, who had been scheduled to speak, announced that if I spoke he would not appear on the same platform. Some parents said they would organize a walkout.

I was visited by a delegation of students, obviously embarrassed. The principal had asked them to ask me to withdraw. I said yes, I would, if they took a poll of the student body and the students— who had invited me in the first place—now wanted me to withdraw. The poll was taken. The students voted overwhelmingly that I should speak.

The day before the ceremony, my wife answered a phone call. The voice at the other end (Roz said it sounded like "a nice old lady") said, "Just tell your husband that my two boys are now out in the garage, building a bomb for the commencement."

The football field where the graduation ceremony took place was ringed by police. The principal, sitting next to me on the platform, was visibly nervous. I don't remember exactly what I said that day (the FBI was not on the job; there was nothing in my file on this event, and I have grown to depend on them for accurate reports on my speeches). But I know I spoke as strongly, as feelingly as I could about the war, the Kent State shootings, the right of young people to refuse to fight in an unjust war.

The stands were full—parents, students, teachers. When I started to speak a handful of parents conspicuously rose and walked out, but when I finished there was a standing ovation. Here, as at other gatherings, it seemed to me that people were grateful when someone voiced openly what they were thinking and feeling but had no way of expressing.

(For years after that I would run into young people who stopped me on the street, or on a bus, saying, "I graduated from Newton North in 1970, and I'll never forget that day." It confirmed what I learned from my Spelman years, that education becomes most rich and alive when it confronts the reality of moral conflict in the world.)

Around this time I was invited to Tufts University to debate William F. Buckley, the well-known writer-columnist-conservative. (I was offered $300, which impressed me; I was accustomed to getting nothing. I learned later that Buckley got $3,000—but I suppressed my resentment.) The Tufts gymnasium was packed that night with thousands of students, and thousands more were turned away. Obviously, it was not my presence but the famous Buckley who was attracting them.

When we were introduced by a Tufts philosophy professor the applause seemed fairly even for both Buckley and myself. As the debate went on, however, the applause diminished for Buckley, grew louder for me. I knew this was not because I was a superior debater, but that my arguments simply made more sense to a student body that had itself decided the war was wrong.

At a certain point I glanced over at Buckley, who had a reputation for debonair coolness, and I saw he was sweating. Before the question period was declared at an end he rose and said he had to go. In a column he wrote after the debate he said how appalled he was that American students should applaud such opposition to their own government as they heard that evening. I found it curious that Buckley did not seem to understand that unsparing criticism of government is an essential element of a democratic society.

"Counter-commencements" were being organized around the country. I spoke at such an event at my alma mater, Columbia University, while the historian who had chaired my dissertation defense, Richard Hofstadter, was giving the official commencement address nearby. At another, at Wesleyan University, I shared the counter-commencement platform with two of my heroes, the historian Henry Steele Commager, who had been my teacher at Columbia, and William Sloane Coffin, with whom I had become friends over the years.

It was a time of incredibly intense passions, as the horrors visited on the people of Vietnam became more known, as the bodies of young Americans were shipped home by the tens of thousands. Perhaps there was a special desperation about what was happening because we felt *we* were in some way responsible. Again and again, since World War II, there had been talk about the responsibility of the German people for the Nazi atrocities. Yet atrocities were now taking place in Vietnam—undoubtedly on both sides, but the most massive firepower was ours, the foreign presence in that country was us. The My Lai massacre was only one instance of the awful things done by our soldiers, and *we*, by our failure to stop the war, were responsible and therefore must act.

For some people it was too much to bear. Norman Morrison, a pacifist father of three, set fire to himself, giving his life to protest the war, as did a woman named Alice Herz. (Later, in North Vietnam, I met Vietnamese peasants whose only English words were "Norman Morrison, Norman Morrison.")

One evening in Boston I got a phone call from Washington, from a student of mine whose anguish about the war had been very visible when he spoke to me after class. He had gone to the Capitol steps earlier that day, doused himself with gasoline, and then been arrested before he could do anything more. (To this day I hear from him once a year or so; he is obviously still troubled. He writes poems, is fearful of police and the FBI, a gentle person still tormented by the violence of the world around him.)

But for most of us, the movement was a life-giving force. To join a hundred thousand others in marches and rallies, to know that even if you felt helpless against the power of government you were not alone in your feelings—that people all over the country, of all ages, black and white, working people and middle-class people, were with you—was to be moved beyond words.

To hear Bob Dylan and Joan Baez and Country Joe and the Beatles, to have artists and writers on your side, to read that Eartha Kitt upset a White House lawn party by raising her voice against the war, to see Mohammed Ali defy the authorities even at the cost of his championship title, to hear Martin Luther King speak out against the war, to see little children marching with their parents, carrying signs—"Save the Children of Vietnam"—was to feel that the best of human beings were fighting your cause.

While we were an embattled minority, it was thrilling to imagine that the beautiful humanity of so many of the people we encountered in the movement (forgetting its dogmatists, its bureaucrats, the power-seekers, the humorless ones) represented the future. It seemed there could be some day a world of just such people, the kind you could work with, share everything with, have fun with, trust with your life.

We often read in the press—or heard from some people—that the opposition to the war came from young people wanting to save their own lives. That was so clearly untrue; millions of people protested the war not because their own lives were at stake, but because they truly cared about *other people's lives*, the lives of Vietnamese, of fellow Americans.

There was no more powerful argument against the claim of selfishness, and no greater inspiration for continuing the struggle to end the war, than to be joined by the GI's themselves—those who refused to go out on patrol, who deserted (perhaps a hundred thousand of them), who were courtmartialed and sent to prison, who came back from the war and chained themselves to the fences of the

Veterans Administration, who marched with their crutches, with their artificial limbs, in their wheelchairs, to cry out against the stupid slaughter.

On army, navy, and air bases in the United States, soldiers getting ready to go to Vietnam joined those back from the war to call for a halt. They put out antiwar newspapers and gathered in movement coffeehouses set up near military bases, where they could listen to music, talk, find an alternative to the bars and the macho militarism they were supposed to enjoy. The first such coffeehouse (called the U.F.O.) opened in Columbia, South Carolina, and our son Jeff, barely out of high school, went there to become part of the working staff as a musician.

I traveled to Mountain Home, Idaho (the FBI recorded this visit), to meet with airmen stationed there who put out an antiwar newspaper called *Helping Hand*. We talked, listened to music, then late at night drove high into the mountains to strip and bathe in the hot springs, under a sliver of moon.

In the spring of 1971 I traveled to Detroit to participate in the "Winter Soldier" hearings—where Vietnam veterans were gathering to give testimony about the atrocities they had witnessed or participated in, actions which had helped turn them against the war. That was the first of several encounters with Jane Fonda. She became the object of "patriotic" venom, but I always admired her willingness to step out of her superstar life to take a stand on the war.

On that occasion I also met the actor Donald Sutherland, who would soon play in a movie based on the book *Johnny Got His Gun*, written by one of the blacklisted Hollywood writers, Dalton Trumbo. This book, perhaps the most powerful antiwar novel ever written, had a profound effect on me when I read it as a teenager— prepared me, I think, for my later revulsion against all war. When I started teaching I often assigned it to my students. I also had them read *Born on the Fourth of July*, the memoir by Ron Kovic, a working-class kid who joined the Marines at seventeen, and at nineteen had his spine shattered by shellfire in Vietnam. Paralyzed from the waist down, in a wheelchair, he came home to become a protester against the war. In his book, Ron Kovic tells how, back from Vietnam, he heard Donald Sutherland read from *Johnny Got His Gun*, and how it crystallized his own feelings.

That chain of relationships made me think of how connections are made—you read a book, you meet a person, you have a single experience, and your life is changed in some way. No act, therefore, however small, should be dismissed or ignored.

One day in the 1980s, I got a phone call in Boston; Ron Kovic was in town, had read some of my work, wanted to meet me. I asked if he would come to my class; the students would be thrilled. He came, but not to lecture the four hundred students in the auditorium. Instead, he wheeled his wheelchair up and down the aisle, asking *them* questions, conveying in his own way how deeply he wanted a world without war, without violence.

After four years of negotiations in Paris, with fifty-five thousand Americans dead, with over a million Vietnamese dead, after the most intense bombardment of a tiny country by a major power in history, after failing at military victory, the United States signed a peace treaty with North Vietnam in early 1973, agreeing to withdraw. The war continued between the Saigon government and the Hanoi–National Liberation Front forces, with the United States continuing to give military aid to Saigon, but a North Vietnamese offensive smashed through the demoralized South Vietnamese army in early 1975.

That April, a teach-in was organized at Brandeis University in the Boston area, to ask for the cessation of U.S. military aid to Saigon. I was on the platform, as I had been so many times during the war, with Noam Chomsky, who had been one of the first American intellectuals, and undoubtedly the most influential, to speak out against the war. His 1967 article in the *New York Review of Books*, "The Responsibility of Intellectuals," was a historic document delivered in a tone of firm rationality, an eloquent call for others to speak up against American policy in Vietnam.

Noam and I had first met in the summer of 1965, on a plane ride to Mississippi with a delegation to protest the jailing of civil rights workers there. The antiwar movement brought us closer together, and Noam and his wife Carol, Roz, and I became friends. Of all the movement people I knew, there was no one person who combined such extraordinary intellectual power with such commitment to social justice.

In the midst of that Brandeis meeting in 1975 (I forget who was at the microphone) there was an interruption. A student came racing down the aisle, waving a piece of paper. He was with the campus newspaper and they had just received the news: Saigon had surrendered, the war was over. Everyone in the auditorium stood and cheered. We shook hands. We embraced. I felt great joy, but perhaps more than anything a sense of relief that the killing had stopped. It was, I suppose, the last teach-in of the war.

There was also an exhilarating feeling of pride, even awe, for, as the great anarchist-journalist I. F. Stone said, it was human beings against technological power, and human beings had won. It was an exciting thought, that apparently powerless people, both in our country and in Vietnam, had confronted the awesome power of the United States government and brought a terrible war to an end. But there is more to say about the antiwar movement—about priests and nuns, about going to Hanoi, about being part of an underground, about being arrested, about jails and courtrooms, about the problem of obedience to law and subservience to government.

"Our Apologies,
Good Friends,
for the Fracture
of Good Order"

On January 30, 1968, I was teaching a seminar in political theory at Boston University when someone came into the room and said he was sorry to interrupt the class, but I was urgently wanted on the telephone. "Can't it wait until I finish my class?" I asked. "The person says he must talk to you now." I asked the students to wait and went quickly to the office to pick up the phone.

On the other end was David Dellinger, one of the national leaders of the antiwar movement, whom I had met in Hiroshima in 1966. He told me that he had received a telegram from the North Vietnamese government in Hanoi, saying they were prepared to make their first release of three captured American pilots, as a peace gesture in honor of the traditional Tet New Year holiday. Would the peace movement send "a responsible representative" to Hanoi to receive the pilots?

Dave and other peace movement leaders thought it would be good for two people to make the trip, and they had already asked Father Daniel Berrigan (I had vaguely heard of him), a Catholic priest and a formidable poet (he had won the distinguished Lamont Prize in poetry) then teaching at Cornell, who had been speaking out against the war. Berrigan was ready to go.

(The Vietnamese had asked for "a responsible representative." Did Berrigan and I, both half-responsible, add up to what was wanted?)

"Well, Howard," Dave asked, "would you be willing to go?"

"When? For how long?"

"Tomorrow. For a week. Maybe two." I thought quickly. My classes: I could get colleagues to cover them. Roz: she would want me to go. I agreed to show up the next morning at an apartment in Manhattan.

I returned to my seminar and told my students what the call was about. They were excited: I was going to the capital city of "the enemy" to bring home three prisoners of war.

The next day, at an apartment in downtown Manhattan, I met Daniel Berrigan, slim, dark-haired, soft-spoken, dressed in black pants, black turtleneck, and sneakers, a silver medallion hanging from his neck. He had an impish wit. I was relieved. I didn't want to spend a lot of close time with someone who believed that fun is a bourgeois indulgence. Dave Dellinger was there, and Tom Hayden, whom I had known for several years. Both were among the few Americans who had visited North Vietnam during the war, and would "brief" me and Dan Berrigan on our trip.

As we talked, a knock on the door. A well-dressed man was there. From the State Department. They had learned about our trip "from intelligence reports," they said (meaning they had read the *New York Times* story on us that morning). Wanted to talk to us before we left. Wanted to stamp our passports to legalize our trip. North Vietnam was on the list of Communist countries where it was illegal to travel. No, we said, we didn't want official approval for our trip from the government we were fiercely opposing for its actions in Vietnam.

On our twenty-eight-hour plane trip, wherever we stopped—Copenhagen, Frankfurt, Teheran, Calcutta, Bangkok—some well-dressed man would come onto the plane. "I'm from the U.S. Embassy. I am prepared to stamp your passports." No, thanks. Dan Berrigan and I were in agreement on that.

It had started as "Father Berrigan," but very quickly it was "Dan," as I got over that psychological obstacle, going back to childhood, when priests were forbidding men in black. We had never met before the day we were to fly out of New York to Vietnam, but we were to spend almost three weeks together in extraordinary circumstances.

Dan came from working-class parents in upstate New York and was ordained a priest in the Jesuit order. In the early sixties he had reacted to the civil rights movement in a way that suggested to the more conservative of the church fathers that he should be sent off to Latin America. The wrong move, Dan said to me, smiling. To see poverty in the police-state atmosphere of Latin America only provoked more strongly his desire to act, no holds barred, on behalf of peace and justice.

When I discovered his poems I was moved by their simplicity, their passion. As I was by the poem he sent to Roz and me years later when Mitch Snyder, the hero of the homeless, died in Washington. It was about those who "stood and stood and stood" and those who "walked and walked and walked":

> Why do you stand
>   they were asked, and
>   Why do you walk?
>
> Because of the children, they said, and
>   because of the heart, and
>   because of the bread.
>
>   Because
>   the cause
>   is the heart's beat
> and the children born
> and the risen bread.

Our arrival in Vientiane, Laos, was supposed to coincide with the arrival of another plane—a creaky World War II aircraft owned by the International Control Commission (about the only thing left of the failed 1954 Geneva Accords ending the French war in Indochina). That plane made six trips a month—from Saigon to Phnompenh, Cambodia, to Vientiane, Laos, to Hanoi—and our trip was timed to connect with one of those.

But the Tet offensive was on in Vietnam that February of 1968. The Viet Cong, supposedly on the run and overwhelmed by the enormous firepower of the United States, had sprung up suddenly all over South Vietnam in a series of surprise attacks, even in Saigon itself, occupying the U.S. embassy at one point. They had made the Tan San Hut airport in Saigon inoperable, and so our plane did not arrive.

Dan and I therefore passed a strange week in Vientiane, in a shabby old hotel on the Mekong River, across from Thailand. Vientiane had the air of World War II Casablanca, a city of spies and drugs and international intrigue. In Vientiane, every major power in the world had an embassy, and after work their attaches mingled in the dark pot-smoking cafes of the city.

The day we arrived, an Asian man (Laotian? Thai? Chinese?) approached us in the lobby of our hotel, speaking French, saying he was with the French news agency, Agence France-Presse, and would like to interview us about our mission to Hanoi. We said maybe later, when we're settled in. Two hours later, another man approached us in the lobby, speaking French: "I'm from Agence France-Presse, and I'd like to talk to you about your trip." We told him a colleague of his had already contacted us. He said, "That's interesting. I'm the only representative of Agence France-Presse in Vientiane."

That week we endlessly walked the streets of Vientiane, and along the bank of the Mekong, waiting for our plane to arrive from Phnompenh. One morning we were awakened by a phone call from someone in the lobby: an American voice, saying he would like to meet us, talk with us. When we went downstairs, there was a tall young man in black pajamas, the attire of the Laotian peasant. This was Fred Branfman, who had been in the Peace Corps in Tanzania and admired its unusual leader, Julius Nyerere. He'd gone back to the States and, opposing the Vietnam war, joined the International Volunteer Service. This was a program that allowed exemption from military service in exchange for overseas work, mostly in rural areas.

Fred lived with a poor family in a village not far from Vientiane. He was happy there, he told us, this fellow from a comfortable middle-class family on Long Island. He took us to a little hut on stilts, introduced us to his "father and mother." He had stopped on the way to pick up some strips of meat, and when it was cooked we all sat in a circle on the floor, dipping into the plates of meat and rice with our fingers, Fred acting as interpreter in our conversation with the middle-aged couple. After we ate, the husband went to a corner where there was a small Buddhist shrine. "He's praying for you," Fred said. "Praying for your safety on your trip." The man came over to us and tied a string around Dan Berrigan's left wrist, then one around mine. Fred explained. "It's to keep danger away." When we parted, bowing, the man and his wife said something to us. Fred interpreted: "They want you to know that they love you." (I kept the string on my wrist for a long time after my trip to Vietnam, until it darkened and frayed and fell apart.)

Finally the word came: the plane was arriving. We would leave in the late afternoon. There was a crowd assembled at the airport to see us off, lots of reporters and photographers. As we prepared to board the plane, a man came out of the crowd. Suit and tie. "I'm from the U.S. Embassy. I'm prepared to validate your passport." We smiled and shook our heads. He hesitated. "Not even orally?" No, thanks.

We flew through the night, at a specified altitude on a specified route, by agreement with the North Vietnamese so that the I.C.C. plane would not be taken for a U.S. bomber. One plane had been shot down by mistake. We were given flak helmets, just in case. But it was a smooth flight, with a planeload mostly of diplomats coming back to their posts in Hanoi.

We flew low over the Red River, saw the pontoon bridge that had been bombed again and again, repaired ingeniously again and again. Upon landing, we were greeted with warm smiles and flowers, then an auto trip through the night to Hanoi, past bombed-out build-ings, antiaircraft crews bunched in the darkness, people on foot and on bicycles moving along the road in an endless, thick stream. We were taken to an old French hotel where we sat, just the two of us, in an enormous dining room, and were served omelettes by tuxe-doed waiters who looked as if they were carryovers from the co-lonial French.

They led us to adjoining rooms, clean and comfortable, with lit-tle trays of candy, cookies, and cigarettes beside the beds. We were both dead tired, but Dan Berrigan stopped me from rushing to my room. He reached into his small knapsack, which was his only trav-eling bag (I thought, does God, like the airlines, have a weight limit for luggage?), pulled out a bottle of cognac, and we both had a few sips before going to bed. This was to be a nightly ritual while we were in Hanoi.

We were awakened after an hour by the sound of sirens wailing through the hotel. An air raid. As we were contemplating what to do, there was a knock at the door. A young girl motioned to us to follow her, and took us down into the air raid shelter under the ho-tel, where sleepy guests from all parts of the world, in various states of undress, sat for the next hour while Hanoi was bombed.

It was a new experience for me—a bombardier now on the re-ceiving end of bombs from the air force I had been a part of. I had that taut feeling in my belly that I remembered from my World War II missions—fear. I thought, I guess I deserve this. No one spoke. We listened to two kinds of sounds: the deep booms of the bombs exploding (were the booms coming closer, were they gradually louder?) and the sharper crack of antiaircraft guns. Then silence, then the all-clear siren, and we went back to our rooms and to sleep.

When we awoke in the morning, Dan Berrigan showed me the poem he had written before going to sleep. Every morning we were in Hanoi, Dan had a new poem to show me that he had written late in the night. I loved those poems.

The week we were there the air raids came every day. Four, five, six times a day the sirens sounded. Wherever we were, with whom-ever we were, we were quietly, efficiently taken to the nearest shelter. In the streets we walked constantly over one-person shelters, cylindrical holes dug into the streets for pedestrians to duck into. I had seen photos of them, taken by *Life* photographer Lee Lockwood, who had managed to get to Hanoi. (Lee later became a good friend.)

We tried to grasp that these people around us had been doing this, responding to air raid sirens, every day for three years. It took me a while to notice it was a city without children—almost all had been evacuated to the countryside to escape the bombs. We visited the zoo one day, and the monkey cages were empty—the monkeys had also been sent to the countryside to keep them safe.

For five days we went about the city with four Vietnamese guides—young, friendly, easy-going. Three of them spoke English, one spoke French. We returned every evening to the hotel to share a drink with them at the bar before saying goodnight. But there was no mention of the prisoners we had presumably come to pick up, and Dan Berrigan and I were beginning to worry (Was the deal off? Had they forgotten what we were there for?) when one evening the one called Oanh, a musician and composer, said to us, "Please eat supper quickly. In one hour we will meet the three prisoners."

We drove through dark streets to the prison—what seemed like an old French villa adapted to its new function. There was the usual introductory tea session. Then the prison commandant read to us his data on the three fliers: Major Norris Overly, thirty-nine, wife and two children in Detroit; Captain John Black, thirty, wife and three kids in Tennessee; Lieutenant Junior Grade David Methany, twenty-four, single. Then the three men emerged, bowed to the commandant, and sat down.

One of our guides whispered to us, "Whether or not you shake hands is up to you." Dan and I walked over and shook hands. We talked. "You fellows are looking good." (They were. Had they been especially well treated for show?) "What's your home town? . . . Oh yes, I know someone in Des Moines . . ." And so on. A strange conversation under the circumstances. Perhaps.

The following day there was a formal ceremony for us to "receive" the prisoners, with the whole international press corps of Hanoi present. There were statements from the Vietnamese and from Dan Berrigan speaking for the two of us, and a few polite words of thanks to the North Vietnamese government from Lieutenant Methany for the fliers.

Then we went back to the hotel, where it had been arranged for us to have supper alone with the three men. An elegant supper, served by a battery of waiters: endless bowls of hot potage, cold cuts, chicken, bread, beer. We had a friendly talk, but we didn't discuss the war. They told us they were wary of us at first (we were from the notorious "peace movement") but felt okay now. It helped, I think, that it was a priest and a former Air Force man who had come for them.

The flight from Hanoi to Vientiane was smooth; the stewardess served candies and aperitifs and we all relaxed. I sat between Major Overly and Captain Black. Dan Berrigan sat with Methany. Overly told me about his experiences in captivity. Shot down, and then, on a twenty-eight-day trek under military guard to Hanoi, threatened and beaten by furious villagers (so many had lost children, parents, loved ones, in the bombings), often saved by the guards.

"It was all strange. One moment someone would want to kill me. The next minute another Vietnamese would act toward me with such compassion that it just staggered me. I had a huge infection on my back and was in great pain. They gave me sulfa, and after a long time it was cured." In prison, Overly said, the worst was over—no maltreatment, no indoctrination, just a few books on Vietnamese history, sufficient food, medical care.

In Laos, the U.S. ambassador arrived and hustled them onto a military plane. We would never see or hear from them again. Later, back in the States, we read that Overly was speaking around the country, telling of maltreatment and torture in prison. I was surprised, because on that plane to Vientiane there had been no reason for him to lie to me about his experience.

Nevertheless, whatever the truth about Overly's own treatment, I cannot doubt the stories of torture and maltreatment that came out of the prison camps after the war. Brutality is not something confined to one or another side of the ideological wars—it is part of the environment of prisons everywhere and should be condemned in every single case.

Dan Berrigan and I made the long flight back to the States, and, very tired, faced batteries of microphones and cameras, then separated. But our trip to Hanoi led to a lifelong friendship.

That friendship would grow, when Dan became an outlaw, and I would help hide him.

In the fall of 1967, Dan Berrigan's brother, Phil Berrigan, once a soldier in World War II, now a priest, had staged a dramatic protest against the war. He and three other men had entered a draft office in Baltimore, removed draft records from the files, and poured blood over them to symbolize the destruction of life in Vietnam. They were arrested and sentenced to prison terms. But their action was to lead to others.

Very soon after our return from Hanoi, Dan Berrigan was shaken by the death of a Catholic teenager who had entered a cathedral in Syracuse, New York, poured kerosene on his body, and set himself afire as a protest against the war. A few months later, Dan and his brother Phil (who was out on bail) joined seven others, including two women, the Maryknoll nun Marjorie Melville and a nurse, Mary Moylan, in entering a draft board in Catonsville, Maryland, removing files, and using home-made napalm to set fire to draft records before being arrested.

The Catonsville Nine thus joined the Baltimore Four, and after that the list of draft board actions would grow (the Milwaukee Fourteen, the Boston Two, the Camden Twenty-eight, and a half-dozen others). They were tried and convicted, but not before they spoke at length and from their hearts to the jury about why they had decided to break the law. In effect, they were putting the war itself on trial.

In advance of the action, Dan Berrigan wrote: "Our apologies, good friends, for the fracture of good order, the burning of paper instead of children. . . . We could not, so help us God, do otherwise. For we are sick at heart, our hearts give us no rest for thinking of the Land of Burning Children. . . . We ask our fellow Christians to consider in their hearts a question which has tortured us, night and day, since the war began. How many must die before our voices are heard, how many must be tortured, dislocated, starved, maddened? . . . When, at what point, will you say no to this war?"

They were sentenced to terms of two to three years, but remained free on bail pending appeal. Those appeals went on for a year and a half, all of them failing, and finally the order went out to pick up the defendants. Three of them could not be found—Mary Moylan, Philip Berrigan, Daniel Berrigan—and the FBI went into a frantic search. (I am only guessing at their mood, judging by their massive effort.)

I received a phone call in early 1970, asking me to come to Ithaca, New York, to speak on the war. I was given no details, but in those years we asked few questions. When I arrived I was met by that extraordinary anarchist intellectual Paul Goodman, who told me about the huge antiwar rally that had just taken place in the Cornell University gymnasium.

It had been rumored that Dan Berrigan would speak, and dozens of FBI agents were mingling with the crowd, ready to pounce on him. On the stage there was a kind of Passover peace ceremony, in the course of which, as is customary at Passover, a door is left open for the prophet Elijah. The door was opened and Dan Berrigan came in, onto the stage. The FBI agents in the crowd rushed toward him, but all the lights went out.

When the lights came on again a few moments later, Berrigan was gone. He had hidden on the stage, inside a huge puppet belonging to the famous Bread and Puppet Theatre group, and was carried out, along with their other giant puppets, onto a waiting truck.

As for my speaking engagement at Ithaca College, antiwar students had arranged for me to collect a $1,000 fee. This would be used to start a fund to support Dan Berrigan while he was underground.

A few days later I received another phone call. (It's easy to understand why phone-tapping is so important to the police.) Would I come to New York to speak on the war at a Catholic Church on the Upper West Side of Manhattan? The priest there was a staunch opponent of the Vietnam intervention, and my friend Eqbal Ahmad, a Pakistani intellectual very active in the movement, would also speak.

I was met at LaGuardia Airport by a young woman, a nun. By this time I was feeling at home with nuns wearing ordinary street clothes, with priests getting married. I was developing great affection for these wonderful men and women who were challenging not just the government of the United States but their own religious hierarchy. The nun told me that Philip Berrigan had just that afternoon been discovered by the FBI in the church apartment of the parish priest; they had smashed down the door and arrested him.

Indeed, the FBI was sure that Dan Berrigan too was in the vicinity and might appear at the church meeting; in the crowd of perhaps five hundred people packed into the church that evening there seemed to be swarms of agents—trench coats, fedoras, the famous Bureau wardrobe—circulating through the audience and around the platform.

On the platform I sat with Eqbal, and with Liz McAlister, the nun who later married Philip Berrigan. (They would have three children in the years to come and all live in a Baltimore peace community where everyone seemed to take turns going to jail for anti-war, anti-militarism protests.) Liz and I had become good friends, and as we sat there she passed me a note for me and Eqbal to meet her after the church rally, at a Spanish-Chinese restaurant farther up Broadway, near Columbia University.

Eqbal and I wended our way (using all the evasive tricks we had learned from the chase scenes in Hollywood movies) to the restaurant. There was Liz and also Sister Joques Egan, a distinguished Catholic educator, former president of Marymount College, who had served forty days in jail for refusing to speak to a grand jury investigating antiwar activists.

The two women told us that Dan Berrigan was hiding out in a house in New Jersey, but that it was not safe. They gave us the address; we were to go there and arrange for him to be moved elsewhere. The next morning, Eqbal and I rented a car, drove to New Jersey, found Dan, and talked over the situation. He said getting out of there was urgent—across the street was the home of an FBI agent. We decided he should come to Boston, where I would be able to work out a secure situation for him.

We found someone to drive him to Boston, and the next evening he turned up at our apartment, the last time he would come there because we knew that I would be high on the list of suspected friends. In our strategy session that night we put together the names of people who would not be on any FBI list as friends of Dan— people who might be willing to harbor him while he was underground. None of us had any idea how long that would last.

We knew that anyone who helped a fugitive was in danger of prison. But none of those we asked to take Dan in—a young editor, an artist and her family, the family of two college professors—refused. He moved from one to the other, became part of each household. A half-dozen of us constituted ourselves as his support committee, arranging to transfer him from place to place, deciding what he could safely do or not do. (He had his own ideas, and often refused to follow our "orders.")

He read, and wrote poetry, but he wanted very much to go to the movies, to take walks along the Charles River, and so we decided to try to disguise him. Someone came up with a wig, which only made him look grotesque and would have made him stand out immediately in any crowd. We had fun one evening as Dan tried it on, in different poses.

One time he needed a tooth repaired, and so I made an appointment with my dentist for a "Mr. McCarthy" who was visiting me from out of town. As we sat in the waiting room, a copy of *Time* magazine was on the table before us. It was opened, and on the page was a story and a photo: "Fugitive Father Daniel Berrigan." But my dentist was not aware. (Years later I told him the truth and he said, "You should have told me; I would have been proud to help.")

That spring, with Dan Berrigan underground, I was teaching my course in political theory at Boston University. In a book I had published two years earlier (*Disobedience and Democracy*) I had discussed the issue of whether a person committing civil disobedience has an obligation to give himself/herself up for punishment.

My own opinion was that there was no such obligation—that to evade prison was to continue the civil disobedience, to continue the protest.

In my class we read Plato's *Crito*, in which Socrates refuses to escape from jail and his death sentence, and defends his decision by saying he has an obligation to do whatever the state tells him to do. In arguing against that, I used the example of Dan Berrigan going underground, continuing to speak out against an unjust war. The class was unaware, of course, that he was right there in Boston.

Dan was underground for four months. But not totally. He would emerge from time to time and quickly disappear, driving the FBI a bit crazy, I'm sure. We arranged for a secret interview in Connecticut with a major network news broadcaster; he appeared in a church in Philadelphia to deliver the Sunday sermon; he became the subject of a documentary by Lee Lockwood, *The Holy Outlaw*. He broadcast messages to the country at the time of the Cambodia invasion and the Kent State killings.

We were proud of our efficiency in keeping him safe. But it was not to last. He insisted, against our suggestion, on visiting two old friends of his, the poets William Stringfellow and Anthony Towne, who had a house on Block Island, a beautiful summer spot in the ocean south of Rhode Island. A letter to his imprisoned brother Phil, telling of his plan to go, was entrusted to a messenger who turned out to be an informant for the FBI. Dan woke one morning and saw men, a surprising number of them, out in the bushes around the house.

Bill Stringfellow went out to inquire. "We're birdwatchers," they explained. Father Daniel Berrigan was the bird they were watching, and they arrested him and took him on a motor launch to the mainland. The sea was rough, and the FBI men with him got sick. There is a funny photograph of Dan handcuffed, an FBI man on either side of him, arriving on the mainland. The captured fugitive has a broad smile on his face; his captors look quite miserable.

PART THREE

Scenes and Changes

In Jail:
"The World Is
Topsy-Turvy"

An encounter with police, even one night in jail, is an intense and unique educational experience. I don't know the exact number of people who were arrested in civil rights and antiwar activities in the sixties and early seventies, but it must have been between fifty thousand and a hundred thousand. (Thirteen thousand were arrested in one day in Washington, D.C.; thousands were arrested in Birmingham alone, a thousand in little Albany, Georgia, and so on.) That means a lot of learning took place.

The learning is about: the nature of the legal system in a liberal democracy (in brief, not so liberal, not so democratic); the willingness of people to give up their freedom for the cause of peace and justice; and the capacity of human beings, when the ordeal of imprisonment demands a concentration on one's own needs, to sacrifice for others.

I conclude all this from what I saw in the South and in the antiwar movement. And also from my own small experience with arrests and jails. (A famous scientist was asked, "How many examples do you need in order to generalize?" He answered, "Two is good, but one will do.")

By the latter part of May 1970, feelings about the war had become almost unbearably intense. In Boston about a hundred of us decided to sit down at the Boston Army Base and block the road used by buses carrying draftees off to military duty. We were not so daft that we thought we were stopping the flow of soldiers to Vietnam; it was a symbolic act, a statement, a piece of guerrilla theatre. We were all arrested and charged, in the quaint language of an old statute, with "sauntering and loitering" in such a way as to obstruct traffic.

Arraigned in court, most of the demonstrators pled guilty, got small fines, and went home. Eight of us insisted on a jury trial, although a jury "of one's peers" is one of the myths of the legal system. A jury is always a more orthodox body than any defendant brought before it; for blacks it is usually a whiter group, for poor people, a more prosperous group.

We were brought to trial about six months later, in November 1970, and represented ourselves in court. We spoke directly to the jury about the war, about what it was doing to Vietnam, about what it was doing to the American people. We talked about how the American political system seemed incapable of stopping a war which was both unconstitutional and immoral. And therefore, how acts of civil disobedience, in the grand tradition of the Boston Tea Party and the antislavery actions, were necessary to speak to the public and the government in a dramatic way.

It didn't seem to matter. As the judge put it to them, the only issue was did we or did we not obstruct traffic? Another lesson about the justice system: the way the judge charges the jury inevitably pushes them one way or the other, limits their independent judgment.

We were found guilty, sentenced to seven days or a twenty-one-dollar fine. Five of the defendants paid the fine. I was ready to do that, too—I had no desire to spend any time in jail. But two of the group—a woman from Wellesley named Vaneski Genouves, and a young fellow from Cambridge, Eugene O'Reilly—said they would go to jail, and I felt I could not desert them, so I also refused to pay the fine. The judge seemed reluctant to have us in jail, so he gave the three of us forty-eight hours to change our minds, after which we should show up in court to either pay the fine or be jailed.

In the meantime, I had been invited to go to Johns Hopkins University to debate with the philosopher Charles Frankel on the issue of civil disobedience. If I showed up in court as scheduled I would have to miss the debate. I decided it would be hypocritical for me, an advocate of civil disobedience, to submit dutifully to the court order and thereby skip out on an opportunity to speak to hundreds of students about civil disobedience.

So, on the day I was supposed to show up in court in Boston, I flew to Baltimore and that evening faced Charles Frankel for our debate. I had been an admirer of his writings, but now, clearly, he was more reluctant to endorse civil disobedience, more respectful of government.

Civil disobedience, as I put it to the audience, was not the problem, despite the warnings of some that it threatened social stability, that it led to anarchy. The greatest danger, I argued, was civil *obedience*, the submission of individual conscience to governmental authority. Such obedience led to the horrors we saw in totalitarian states, and in liberal states it led to the public's acceptance of war whenever the so-called democratic government decided on it.

My talk began like this: "I start from the supposition that the world is topsy-turvy. . . . Daniel Berrigan is in jail—a Catholic priest, a poet who opposes the war—and J. Edgar Hoover is free. David Dellinger, who has opposed war ever since he was this high . . . is in danger of going to jail. And the men who are responsible for the My Lai massacre are not on trial; they are in Washington serving various functions, primary and subordinate, that have to do with the unleashing of massacres, which surprise them when they occur."

In such a world, I said, the rule of law maintains things as they are. Therefore, to begin the process of change, to stop a war, to establish justice, it may be necessary to break the law, to commit acts of civil disobedience, as Southern blacks did, as antiwar protesters did.

I was at the Washington airport early the next morning, to return to Boston, where I planned to meet my eleven o'clock class. I phoned Roz, who told me, "The news on the radio says you cannot be located and there's a warrant out for your arrest." Again, I would have felt foolish, skipping my class on "Law and Justice in America," in which civil disobedience was one of our topics of discussion, in order to submit to the court. I always believed that teachers taught more by what they *did* than by what they said. I thought, I'm not going to do anything heroic, I'm not going underground, but if the authorities want me they'll have to come for me.

From the Boston airport I went directly to my class. The students were wide-eyed. "You're wanted by the police! Aren't you supposed to turn yourself in?" I said I would, after class. But there was no need for me to do anything. When the class ended and I walked outside, two detectives were waiting for me, with a university official there, too, clearly nervous.

I was brought before the judge, given my chance to pay my fine. I refused and was immediately handcuffed and taken to the Charles Street Jail. This was a holding place for people awaiting trial or serving short sentences—an old dungeon of a building, long ago condemned as unfit even for prisoners. My cellmate was a teenager, a taciturn fellow, there on some drug charge.

That night, in my cell, I didn't get much sleep. The talk, sometimes shouts and screams, in the cellblock, the lights on all night, the cockroaches racing around my bunk, the constant clanging of steel doors. I made up my mind: not one more night. I would pay the rest of my fine and get out of there. Besides, my cellmate thought there was something wrong with me when he learned I could get out by paying a few dollars and chose to stay. Also, I had an engagement in Oregon to talk about the war. And—maybe above all—the cockroaches!

The next morning we were allowed out of our cells into the corridor for something like breakfast. We sat at long tables and were served by other prisoners something that looked like slabs of plywood painted yellow. It was French toast. With something like coffee.

As I ate I heard a guard call my name. I looked up. "Zinn, we got a telegram for you." The other prisoners looked up. People don't receive telegrams in the Charles Street Jail. I took it, somewhat embarrassed. It was signed by two people whose names I recognized; they were new neighbors who had just bought a house next to the two-family where we rented the top apartment. They were from the Midwest, "Middle America," a lawyer and an artist. We didn't know much about them. The message was, "Best wishes. We are on your side." That made up for the French toast.

When U.S. involvement in Vietnam first escalated, in August of 1965, 61 percent of the American people approved of U.S. intervention there. By the spring of 1971, public opinion had turned around dramatically; 61 percent now thought the war was wrong. In late April of 1971, several thousand antiwar veterans converged on Washington, to camp out, to lobby. As one of them said, "It's the first time in this country's history that the men who fought a war have come to Washington to demand its halt while the war is still going on."

In the final event of the veterans' Washington encampment, a thousand of them, many in wheelchairs or on crutches, tossed their medals over a fence that the police had built around the Capitol steps to keep them away. As they did so, one by one, they made personal statements. One of them said, "I'm not proud of these medals. I'm not proud of what I did to receive them. I was in Vietnam for a year and . . . we never took one prisoner alive." An Air Force man said that what he had done was a disservice to his country. "As far as I'm concerned, I'm now serving my country."

The day after the medals were given back, there was a giant antiwar rally in Washington, of perhaps half a million people. It was a peaceful, non-disruptive gathering.

They had barely returned home when a few days later twenty thousand protesters came to Washington prepared to disrupt traffic.

Some spoke, extravagantly, of "shutting down the city." Everyone felt that more than speeches were required to stop the war. Affinity groups were formed, each with a dozen or so people who knew and trusted one another. The idea was to avoid centralized, bureaucratic organization; the members of the affinity group would decide for themselves how to play a part in the overall strategy.

Our affinity group was not one you would think appropriate for guerrilla action in the streets of Washington: Noam Chomsky; Dan Ellsberg, a former marine and government man, his role in releasing the top-secret Pentagon Papers not yet public; Marilyn Young, a historian; Zee Gamson, a woman who taught at the University of Michigan; Fred Branfman, back from Laos and working full-time against the war; Mark Ptashne, a Harvard professor and biologist; Cynthia Frederick, an organizer; Mitch Goodman, a writer and codefendant with Dr. Ben Spock in the trial of the Boston Five.

We assembled too late to join the large march to the Pentagon, and rather than rush to catch up, we decided to act on our own, to block traffic on a main thoroughfare. As we huddled in the middle of the street, we could see the police moving toward us (we had no idea at the time of the numbers mobilized by the government: five thousand police, fifteen hundred National Guardsmen, ten thousand federal troops, including paratroopers). They fired tear gas shells and soon we were enveloped in a cloud of gas. We ran, then reassembled and went out to block another street. This went on for a while. Truth is, symbolic actions (we were not accomplishing anything by blocking the street) always feel a little bizarre.

At one of these regroupings we were bunched on a corner, talking to a passerby who asked to know what was going on. As we spoke, a policeman came up quickly to us and sprayed mace directly into Dan Ellsberg's face, then into mine, and walked away. Dan and I were blinded for about ten minutes. We recovered, but our action was over.

I spent that night with a friend in Washington, and awoke the next morning to find the city under military occupation. I walked to DuPont Circle, and saw it was crowded with GI's of the 101st Airborne Division. I kept walking. Policemen were everywhere.

Just ahead of me I spotted a small group of young fellows—long hair, grungy clothes, unmistakably part of the antiwar actions going on in the city. They were ambling along happily, singing "America the Beautiful." Suddenly the police descended on them, declared them under arrest, and had them spread-eagled against a police car.

It was clear that they were being arrested not for something they had done, but for who they were and how they looked. Without thinking, just responding to my immediate indignation, I stopped and said to the officer standing over one of the fellows, "Why are you arresting them?" (I knew it was a naive and pointless question, and yet I couldn't watch this silently.) The policeman immediately turned to me. "You're under arrest too. Get over there!"

As I was pushed against a police car, a young man came along with a camera and tried to photograph all of this. He was grabbed too, and put under arrest. The bunch of us were pushed into a paddy wagon and driven off. I spent a night in a tiny cell crowded with ten young fellows, many of them eighteen or nineteen, from Wisconsin and California and Georgia and Tennessee. About fourteen thousand people were arrested in Washington those first few days in May, for demonstrating against the war.

I returned to Boston in time to speak at a huge rally, fifty thousand people gathered on the Boston Common. I talked about the necessity for civil disobedience in the face of the failure of the regular mechanisms of government—the electoral process, Congress, the Supreme Court—to stop the war. Civil disobedience was a dramatic way of representing the intense antiwar feelings of a large part of the American public, I said; it therefore, even when violating the law in a technical sense, was a supremely *democratic* act, in accord with the provision in the Bill of Rights for citizens to "petition the government for a redress of grievances."

The following day several thousand of us sat down in an encirclement of the J.F.K. Federal Building. The police were out in force. One of them called to me—a friendly greeting. A jovial, middle-aged man, he had heard me recently give a lecture at Northeastern University to an audience of police officers on the subject of police brutality. Police, I learned over the years, are like soldiers, normally good-natured people, but part of a culture of obedience to orders and capable of brutal acts against anyone designated as "the enemy"—in this case, the antiwar movement.

It was a sunny spring day, and we sat in that great circle, occasionally singing and chanting antiwar slogans. Suddenly the police charged into the circle and yanked certain of the demonstrators out of the crowd into the building. I was one of them. They knocked me around a bit, tore my clothes, threw me into an elevator with a few other demonstrators, and took us upstairs to place us under arrest. I still have the notations I made: "Steven Bertolino, seated next to wife, clubbed on leg, kicked in balls. . . . Guy near him, O'Brien, not doing anything, clubbed on head. Mike Ansara, sitting next to me on floor in elevator, hit by cop, bloody lip."

Later, those arrested were held in a lockup behind the municipal court, waiting to be arraigned. A man named John White pulled a little flute from his pocket and played an Irish jig while two people danced.

In the next several years I was arrested a few more times. Once, a group of us refused to move from the White House lawn, where we'd gathered to protest U.S. support for the murderous government in El Salvador. We were arrested, our hands tied behind our backs with plastic cord (it was a group of religious pacifists committed to nonviolence, but police procedures don't allow for exceptions). We were packed together in an airless paddy wagon for hours, in the suffocating heat of early July. We were soon drenched in sweat and it was harder and harder to breathe. One man passed out and we started to yell; a policeman opened the van door to let in some air.

In the wagon with us was a young black man with long braids, a graduate student in mathematics at Princeton and also, it turned out, a Houdini of sorts. In the wagon, his hands tied together behind him, he used two quick motions to get his hands miraculously in front of him, then used his teeth to loosen the plastic wire. The following day, when we were all in handcuffs in another van, being transported from jail to court, he held up his hands for us to see—no more handcuffs. He didn't talk very much, so I imagined him always thinking, planning his next trick.

It was a long night in the D.C. jail. My cellmate was a small, thin black man in his sixties who didn't touch his food; he had been arrested, he told me, after a violent argument with a friend over money owed. He had a great knob of bone on his knee. It came, he told me, from a lifetime of kneeling to pick cotton in North Carolina.

I lay back on my bunk and thought about people I love, and how lucky I was to be white and not poor and just passing briefly through a system which is a permanent hell for so many. Roz, who was arrested at the Pentagon in a women's antiwar demonstration, told me that her thoughts, spending that night in a cell, were similar—how privileged she was compared to the other prisoners, mostly nonwhite, all poor.

My few brief times in jail were to have an impact the rest of my life. They gave me the smallest of glimpses into the ordeal of the long-term prisoners I came to know.

One of these was Jimmy Barrett, whom I visited every week while he was in the Charles Street Jail in the early seventies. A Boston street kid, he had killed a local thug who was sexually brutalizing him. Jimmy was sentenced to a life term, was committed to the worst of prisons, but never let that destroy him. He became a reader and a remarkable writer. He organized inmate protests against the Vietnam War, and arranged a prisoner fast to donate food to starving people in Africa. Every time I saw him he greeted me with a great smile and an ebullient spirit.

I think also of Tiyo Attallah Salah-el, a black man and a gifted musician, who earned several degrees while in prison, and is writing his autobiography. After corresponding with him for years, I visited him in a Pennsylvania penitentiary, and he leaped out of his seat to hug me, to tell me what he was doing and how he was resigned to live the rest of his life in prison but would not surrender to it, would play music and write and make the abolition of prisons his cause.

I sat in on a court of appeals hearing for a new trial for Jimmy Barrett, the outcome obvious. Judges and parole boards, shuffling through legal briefs and probation reports, remain totally ignorant of the human beings behind those papers.

Over the years I have made many visits to prisoners, including a day spent in Block Nine, the maximum-security cell block of the notorious Walpole prison in Massachusetts. I have taught classes in several prisons. I am convinced that imprisonment is a way of pretending to solve the problem of crime. It does nothing for the victims of crime, but perpetuates the idea of retribution, thus maintaining the endless cycle of violence in our culture. It is a cruel and useless substitute for the elimination of those conditions—poverty, unemployment, homelessness, desperation, racism, greed—which are at the root of most *punished* crime. The crimes of the rich and powerful go mostly unpunished.

It must surely be a tribute to the resilience of the human spirit that even a small number of those men and women in the hell of the prison system survive it and hold on to their humanity.

In Court: "The Heart of the Matter"

I have sat, by now, in dozens of courtrooms, occasionally as a defendant, but mostly as a witness in someone else's trial. I have learned a great deal. The courtroom is one instance of the fact that while our society may be liberal and democratic in some large and vague sense, its moving parts, its smaller chambers—its classrooms, its workplaces, its corporate boardrooms, its jails, its military barracks—are flagrantly undemocratic, dominated by one commanding person or a tiny elite of power.

In courtrooms judges have absolute power over the proceedings. They decide what evidence will be allowed, what witnesses will be permitted to testify, what questions can be asked. Further, the judge is most likely a political appointee or someone elected through a political party, and almost always a fairly prosperous white male, whose background is one of privilege, whose ideas are moderately conservative or moderately liberal.

But the American courtroom is also a place where people, against great odds, may challenge the authority that threatens to imprison them, where some lawyers, judges, and juries occasionally

stand apart from their colleagues and act according to their conscience. Because of these possibilities, the movement against the
Vietnam War was carried out not only in the streets, in auditoriums,
in church meetings, and on the battlefield itself, but in courtrooms
around the country.

In 1968, shortly after I had returned from Vietnam with Daniel
Berrigan, I was called to Milwaukee to testify in the case of the Milwaukee Fourteen. The Fourteen were priests, nuns, and laypeople
who had gone into a draft board, taken thousands of its documents,
and burned them in a symbolic protest against the war.

They were arrested, charged with theft and arson. I was summoned by the defense as an "expert witness"—to put the act in con-
text, to tell the judge and jury that what these people had done was
part of a long tradition of civil disobedience in American history,
that it was not an ordinary "crime" but a form of protest engaged
in by conscientious citizens when traditional modes of expression
are ineffective in righting some wrong.

An expert witness must first have his credentials approved by the
court, and so the lawyer for the Milwaukee Fourteen began by asking me questions about my education and my writings, to "qualify"
me.

He then began his direct examination by asking me to explain the
principles of civil disobedience. I spoke of the Declaration of Independence and its insistence that when a government becomes destructive of basic human rights (the Declaration says "all men" are
created equal, not just Americans, and therefore the basic human
rights of Vietnamese peasants are also our concern) it is the right of
the people to "alter or abolish it." And if they can alter or abolish
it, they can certainly commit civil disobedience against it, as these
defendants had done. I told of Henry David Thoreau's decision to
break the law in protest against our invasion of Mexico in 1846, and
began to give a brief history of civil disobedience in the United
States.

Judge Larsen had had enough. He pounded his gavel and said,
"You can't discuss that. This is getting to the heart of the matter!"

He was right. Courtrooms are not places where one is allowed to get to the heart of the matter.

The lawyer for the Milwaukee Fourteen went on to other questions. "Can you explain to the jury, Dr. Zinn, what is the difference between law and justice?" (A dangerous question; what could be getting more "to the heart of the matter"?) The prosecuting attorney objected to the question. The judge said, "Sustained." More questions about civil disobedience. More objections, all sustained.

I was feeling frustrated. Trial testimony was so often trivial and boring; it seemed that the more fundamental the issue, the less likely that it could be aired in court. I turned to the judge (I knew this was improper, but my reason for being there was to attest to the value of impropriety in a democracy) and asked, in a voice loud enough for everybody in the court to hear, "Why can't I say something important? Why can't the jury hear something important?"

The judge was angry. He said, "You are not permitted to speak out like that. If you do that once more I will have you put in jail for contempt of court." I responded, "An IBM machine could make this decision if the question is only did they do this." The judge rapped his gavel again, more forcefully. I could have gone on, I suppose, dramatically adding my civil disobedience to that of the defendants, but my courage stopped at that point. I must confess that my revolutionary ardor has often been limited by my desire to get home to my wife and kids.

The judge told the jury, "This is a case about arson and theft." He did not want the jury to hear about *why* these people had burned draft records. He did not want to hear about the war in Vietnam. He wanted the jury to treat the defendants as ordinary criminals who for some mysterious purpose had decided to destroy government documents. And so the jury, their judgments limited in this way by the court, found the defendants guilty. They were sentenced to several years in prison.

The judge had permitted the defendants, as is accepted in the field of criminal law, to tell of their "state of mind" when they acted as they did. In this way, some of them managed to give the jury some sense of the moral anguish that led them to break the law. A young priest, Father Bob Cunnane, whom I knew slightly from the Boston area, told how he had been affected by reading Gordon Zahn's book *German Catholics and Hitler's Wars.* "I'd never be here if not for that book. SS troops would go to mass and then go out and collect Jews."

The prosecutor objected. The judge sustained. "Hitler's treatment of Jews is not relevant here."

"But that's why *I'm* here," Cunnane said.

On the plane ride home to Boston, a middle-aged man next to me, short, strong-looking, started a conversation. He told me he worked as a longshoreman on the Boston docks and that he had seen me in the courtroom. What was he doing there? I asked. "My son was on trial." His son was Jim Harney, a priest, one of the Milwaukee Fourteen. He said, "I'm proud that he stood up for what he believes in." (Twenty years later, Jim Harney, long since out of prison, was making regular trips to El Salvador to work with peasants who were resisting the death squads.)

As the Vietnam War went on, and public opinion against the war mounted, juries became more independent, and judges gave them more leeway in considering the broader issues of the war. The Camden Twenty-Eight destroyed draft records, too, but their trial, in 1973 in New Jersey, went quite differently.

Many of them were young Catholics from working-class neighborhoods in Philadelphia. They decided to use movement lawyers from the city as consultants, but to act as their own counsel—a "pro se" defense.

They called to the witness stand an army major formerly in charge of the New Jersey induction center. He described in detail how the draft system discriminated systematically against the poor, the black, the uneducated, and how it regularly gave medical exemptions to the sons of the wealthy. Asked by the prosecutor if he thought private citizens had the right to break into buildings to destroy draft files, he replied, "Probably today, if they plan another raid, I might join them."

One of the defendants, Kathleen (Cookie) Ridolfi, perhaps twenty-one years old, phoned me to ask if I would come to Camden to testify for them. She had read my book *Disobedience and Democracy* and wanted the judge and jury to hear my views.

The judge allowed me, in response to her questions, to speak to the jury about the war. I was able to quote at length from the once secret Pentagon Papers to show how the government had deceived the American people about the nature of the war. I contrasted the public statements by government officials about how U.S. forces had been sent to Vietnam to protect "liberty" and "democracy" and "self-determination" with the secret memos of the National Security Council, in which, discussing the importance of Southeast Asia, they came back again and again to three words: tin, rubber, oil.

Seventeen years later (sometime in 1990), when I was speaking in a Midwestern city, a man came up to me and said we had met before. He was Bob Good, one of the Camden Twenty-Eight. He told me that while I had been testifying, his mother had broken down and had to be led from the courtroom. The day after my testimony, she had taken the stand on behalf of the Camden Twenty-Eight. Bob Good handed me a transcript of what she told the court that day.

Elizabeth Good told how she and her husband, a carpenter, lived on a farm and raised ten children, and how they lost a son in an auto accident. When another son, Paul, was drafted, she, a devout Catholic, was sure God would not take a second child from her. But one day she saw an army officer coming up her driveway, and she knew her son was dead.

It was after that, she said, that her son Bob "seemed to get more concerned—all of us did—about this war in Vietnam. . . . And I still, even until last Friday—I still tried to hang on to that theory that my boy died for his country. But after Mr. Zinn was on the stand, and he spelled it out, 'tin, rubber, and oil,' that's when I broke down. . . .

"The only members of my family—my sisters and brothers that

have died—have died of cancer. And there is a hundred thousand dollars going to be spent for the research of cancer, and seventy billion for defense. Where are our priorities?

"I don't think there was any mother within five hundred miles of our home that was more anti-Communist than I was. . . . Every time the boys tried to talk, I brought in Communism. And this is the way all of us are. . . . I can't understand what we're doing over there. We should get out of this. But not one of us, not a one of us raised our hands to do anything about it. We left it up to these people"—she pointed to the defendants—"for them to do it. And now we are prosecuting them for it. God!"

There was no question but that the defendants had done exactly what the prosecution charged; they had entered a federal building illegally in the night and destroyed draft records. But the jury came back with a verdict of not guilty, and one of the jurors threw a party for the defendants.

That same year, 1973, I was called to Los Angeles to testify in another trial connected with the war—the Pentagon Papers trial of Daniel Ellsberg and Anthony Russo.

I had met Dan Ellsberg four years earlier, when we spoke from the same platform at an antiwar meeting. Noam Chomsky had told me about him: "an interesting man," Ellsberg had a doctorate from Harvard in economics, had been in the Marines, in the State Department and the Defense Department. He had gone to Vietnam, and what he'd seen there had turned him against the war. He was now a research fellow at M.I.T.

Over the next months, he and I and his wife, Pat, and Roz became friends. One evening when the four of us were having coffee in their Cambridge apartment near Harvard Square, Dan said he had to tell us something in strict confidence. When he'd been with the Rand Corporation, a "think tank" for the Defense Department, he had helped put together a secret report, an official history of the Vietnam War.

Going over the internal documents, it was clear to him that the United States had lied again and again to the American people. He decided that the papers constituted a history that the public had a right to know. As one of the top scholars on the project, he was given clearance to take them home. He enlisted the aid of a friend, former Rand researcher Anthony Russo, in a bold plan to photo-copy and release to the public all seven thousand pages, each of which was stamped "Top Secret."

They found a friend who ran an advertising agency and had a copying machine. After the agency closed up shop at five, Dan and Tony went to work, making multiple copies of what became known as the Pentagon Papers. Sometimes Dan's teenage kids, Robert and Mary, would help, methodically crossing out the words "Top Secret" on every page.

They worked late into the night (this was the fall of 1969) for weeks. Once, after midnight, a policeman, seeing the office lighted, came upstairs. They explained, "We're doing some photocopying." He left.

Copies of the Pentagon Papers were then sent to certain senators and members of Congress known to be against the Vietnam War, asking them to publicize the document. None of them would do it. The idea of "classified information," the words "Top Secret," had become something sacred in the almost hysterical atmosphere of the Cold War, and now, in a real war.

"Would you be interested in seeing some of the papers?" Dan asked. He went to a closet and gave me a pile of documents. For the next several weeks I kept them in my office, out of sight, reading them whenever I had some privacy. I had thought that by this time I knew a good deal about the history of U.S. policy in Vietnam, but there were revelations here that were startling, facts that we in the peace movement had claimed as true but only now found corrob-orated, in these documents, by the government itself.

Dan had given a copy to Neil Sheehan, a *New York Times* re-porter he had met in Vietnam. But months had passed and nothing had happened.

One Saturday evening in June 1971, Dan and Pat and Roz and I planned to go to a movie. When they arrived at our place in New-ton, Dan was clearly agitated. He had just phoned someone at the *Times* (not Neil Sheehan) about some matter, and been told that this was not a good time to talk because something odd was happening; the *Times* had put security guards all around the building and the presses were going full blast for the Sunday edition, printing some top-secret government document.

"You should be happy," we told Dan. "They're finally doing it."

"Yes, but I'm pissed off—they should have told me."

The next morning's *New York Times* carried a large headline running across four columns: "Vietnam Archive: Pentagon Study Traces 3 Decades of Growing U.S. Involvement." The story itself covered six pages of commentary and documents. It did not say where the *Times* had secured the material, and it took several days before the FBI traced it to Daniel Ellsberg. But Dan was out of sight, underground (actually, housed by various friends in Cambridge), and distributing more copies of the Pentagon Papers to the *Washington Post* and the *Boston Globe* while the Nixon administration was asking the federal courts to stop publication on grounds of "national security."

Twelve days later, Dan turned himself in at Post Office Square in Boston, where a large crowd of supporters, journalists, and curious onlookers watched as the FBI, somewhat embarrassed because it had not been able to find him, saw him emerge from a car and took him into custody.

Two weeks after the *New York Times* story appeared, the Nixon administration lost its last appeal before the Supreme Court. The majority of the court found that the First Amendment prohibited "prior restraint," that is, stopping any publication in advance. Some members of the Court pointed out, however, that *after* publication, criminal charges would be possible, and so the administration went to work.

Dan Ellsberg was indicted by a grand jury in Los Angeles on eleven different counts, including theft and violation of the Espionage Act—giving to unauthorized persons documents whose disclosure would endanger the national defense. The possible penalty on all these counts added up to a hundred and thirty years in prison. Tony Russo was also indicted, on three counts adding up to forty years in prison.

Their trial took place in federal court in Los Angeles in early 1973. The government placed in evidence eighteen volumes of the Pentagon Papers, and put on the witness stand various high-ranking military men and government officials to testify that maintaining the secrecy of these papers was vital to national security.

Ellsberg and Russo were represented by an extraordinary team of lawyers: Leonard Boudin, a distinguished civil liberties attorney whose experience in defending political dissidents went back to the McCarthy era; Leonard Weinglass, a movement lawyer who had been one of the counsel in the Chicago conspiracy trial coming out of the 1968 Democratic convention; and Charles Nesson, a young professor from Harvard Law School.

They decided to put on the stand two different kinds of witnesses. First they would seek the testimony of former government officials and academics of impeccable respectability—Arthur Schlesinger, Theodore Sorenson, McGeorge Bundy, John Kenneth Galbraith—who would testify on the technical issues of whether the Pentagon Papers contained information injurious to the national defense.

Secondly, they would call "expert witnesses" who themselves had been active against the war and would try to convey to the jury the *moral* issues involved, to use the Pentagon Papers to talk to the jury about the nature of the war: Noam Chomsky, Richard Falk (an expert in international law at Princeton), Tom Hayden, Don Luce (who had spent nine years in Vietnam as a civilian working with Vietnamese peasants), and myself.

It was decided that I would be the first such witness, and so I flew to Los Angeles. I spent the next week reading through the first five volumes of the eighteen which were the government exhibit, to prepare my testimony. In the meantime, I stayed in attorney Len Weinglass's oceanfront house, took long walks on the beach, had Chinese dinners with Dan and Tony, spent an evening in a local club to hear two of my favorite jazz and blues musicians, Sonny Terry and Brownie McGee.

A few days before I was to be called, the defense team brought in Professor Arthur Kinoy of the Rutgers University Law School, for a strategy session. Kinoy was a kind of father-figure to movement lawyers of the sixties, a brilliant legal tactician and veteran of many civil liberties struggles, who had once been dragged out of a hearing of the House Committee on Un-American Activities as he defiantly defended a client.

I sat in on that meeting and it was an education. The various lawyers were going over the technicalities of the indictment: how would they prove that the taking of the Pentagon Papers was not really a theft in the legal sense? Kinoy, a short, wiry, restless dynamo of a man, waved his hand. "No! No! Forget the technicalities!" He clenched his fist. "You need to do just one thing: persuade those twelve people on the jury that Dan Ellsberg and Tony Russo *were right in what they did."*

When I took the stand on a Friday afternoon, I had before me the five volumes of the Pentagon Papers I had been studying. "Will you tell the jury," Len Weinglass said, "what is in those volumes."

The jury was seated a few feet from me. Ten of the twelve were women, of whom at least three were black and one an immigrant from Australia. Of the two men, one was a black man, an official of a local auto union. The other was a wounded marine veteran of Vietnam.

I turned to face them, and in response to a single question from Len Weinglass I spoke for the next few hours on the history of the Vietnam War. It was like teaching a class, but with much more at stake.

My job was to trace the story of U.S. involvement from World War II to 1963. In that year, the American government, seeing the South Vietnamese leader Ngo Dinh Diem unable to suppress a popular rebellion, supported a military coup which overthrew him and executed him. The Pentagon Papers showed the involvement of the United States in that coup, but Henry Cabot Lodge, then the American ambassador to Saigon, who was in constant touch with the plotters, later told reporters, "We had nothing whatsoever to do with it."

"Are you finished?" Len Weinglass asked.

"Yes."

"Now, will you tell the jury, having read those volumes, whether, if made known to the public, they would or would not have injured the national defense?"

I explained that there was nothing in the papers of military significance that could be used to harm the defense of the United States, that the information in them was simply *embarrassing* to our government because what was revealed, in the government's own interoffice memos, was how it had lied to the American public.

I discussed the concept of "national defense," and suggested that a proper definition of the term was defense of the people, not of special interests. The secrets disclosed in the Pentagon Papers might embarrass politicians, might hurt the profits of corporations wanting tin, rubber, oil, in far-off places. But this was not the same as hurting the nation, the people.

The prosecutor chose not to cross-examine me on the documents. He wanted only to show that I was a friend of Daniel Ellsberg. He held a police photo up to the jury and asked me to identify it. It was a photo taken in Boston, at the 1971 demonstration at the federal building, and showed me and Dan Ellsberg sitting together in the crowd.

"No more questions."

There was more testimony that week. Then summations and the judge's charge. The jury was still deliberating, days later, when the judge called it back into the courtroom. The Watergate scandals were coming to light. The Nixon administration had engaged in illegal wiretaps. In an attempt to discredit Dan Ellsberg, it had sent a team to burglarize the files of his psychiatrist. It had even sent men to beat him up when he spoke at an antiwar rally. Based on a number of such illegalities, the judge declared a mistrial. The case of the Pentagon Papers was ended.

The members of the jury were interviewed afterwards, and it was clear that Dan Ellsberg and Tony Russo would not have been convicted.

In the eighties, with the Vietnam War ended, and the press pronouncing the sixties over and the antiwar movement dead, determined groups of activists still engaged in acts of civil disobedience, protesting against military aid to El Salvador and other dictator-ships, against the swollen arms budget, against the immense accumulation of nuclear weapons.

As I testified in a number of these trials, I was encouraged. Where judges allowed juries to hear the full reasons for acts of civil disobedience, were willing to let witnesses get to "the heart of the matter," juries often gave surprising verdicts.

In 1984, I testified in a trial in Burlington, Vermont, where the Winooski Forty-Four had sat in the corridor outside Senator Stafford's office and refused to move. They were protesting his support for the military dictatorship in El Salvador.

Judge Mahady allowed me to discuss the idea of civil disobedience and to tell about its efficacy in bringing about important change in the history of the United States. He allowed testimony from two Salvadoran women whose families and friends had been murdered by government death squads. He allowed ex-CIA agent John Stockwell to tell how the CIA directed American policy in Central America in such a way as to destroy the possibilities for democracy.

The jury voted to acquit all the defendants. Later, one of the jurors said, "I was honored to be on that jury. I felt a part of history."

No doubt the odds are against dissenters in any nation's judicial system. But human beings are not machines, and however powerful the pressure to conform, they sometimes are so moved by what they see as injustice that they dare to declare their independence. In that historical possibility lies hope.

Growing Up
Class-Conscious

I was in my teens when I wrote this poem:

Go see your Uncle Phil
And say hello.
Who would walk a mile today
To say hello,
The city freezing in the snow?

Phil had a news stand
Under the black El.
He sat on a wooden box
In the cold and in the heat.
And three small rooms across the street.

Today the wooden box was gone,
On top the stand Uncle Phil was curled,
A skeleton inside an Army coat.
He smiled and gave me a stick of gum
With stiffened fingers, red and numb.

Go see your Uncle Phil today
My mother said again in June

I walked the mile to say hello
With the city smelling almost sweet
Brand new sneakers on my feet.

The stand was nailed and boarded tight
And quiet in the sun.
Uncle Phil lay cold, asleep,
Under the black El, in a wooden box
In three small rooms across the street.

I recall these lines, certainly not as an example of "poetry," but because they evoke something about my growing up in the slums of Brooklyn in the thirties, when my father and mother in desperate moments turned to saviors: the corner grocer, who gave credit by writing down the day's purchases on a roll of paper; the kind doctor who treated my rickets for years without charging; Uncle Phil, whose army service had earned him a newsstand license and who loaned us money when we had trouble paying the rent.

Phil and my father were two of four brothers, Jewish immigrants from Austria, who came to this country before the First World War and worked together in New York factories. Phil's fellow workers kept questioning him: "Zinn, Zinn—what kind of name is that? Did you change it? It's not a Jewish name." Phil told them no, the name had not been changed, it was Zinn and that's all there was to it. But he got tired of the interrogations and one day had his name legally changed to Weintraub, which from then on was the name of that branch of the family.

My father, looking to escape the factory, became a waiter, mostly at weddings, sometimes in restaurants, and a member of Local 2 of the Waiters Union. While the union tightly controlled its membership, on New Year's Eve, when there was a need for extra waiters, the sons of the members, called juniors, would work alongside their fathers, and I did too.

I hated every moment of it: the ill-fitting waiter's tuxedo, borrowed from my father, on my lanky body, the sleeves absurdly short (my father was five-foot-five and at sixteen I was a six-footer); the way the bosses treated the waiters, who were fed chicken wings just before they marched out to serve roast beef and filet mignon to the guests; everybody in their fancy dress, wearing silly hats, singing "Auld Lang Syne" as the New Year began and me standing there in my waiter's costume, watching my father, his face strained, clear his tables, feeling no joy at the coming of the New Year.

When I first came across a certain e.e. cumming's poem, I didn't fully understand why it touched me so deeply, but I knew it connected with some hidden feeling.

> my father moved through dooms of love
> through sames of am through haves of give,
> singing each morning out of each night
> my father moved through depths of height . . .

His name was Eddie. He was always physically affectionate to his four boys, and loved to laugh. He had a strong face, a muscular body, and flat feet (due, it was said, to long years as a waiter, but who could be sure?), and his waiter friends called him "Charlie Chaplin" because he walked with his feet splayed out—he claimed he could balance the trays better that way.

In the Depression years the weddings fell off, there was little work, and he got tired of hanging around the union hall, playing cards, waiting for a job. So he became at different times a window cleaner, a pushcart peddler, a street salesman of neckties, a W.P.A. worker in Central Park. As a window cleaner, his supporting belt broke one day and he fell off the ladder onto the concrete steps of a subway entrance. I was perhaps twelve and I remember him being brought, bleeding, into our little flat. He had hurt himself badly. My mother would not let him clean windows again.

All his life he worked hard for very little. I've always resented the smug statements of politicians, media commentators, corporate executives who talked of how, in America, if you worked hard you would become rich. The meaning of that was if you were poor it was because you hadn't worked hard enough. I knew this was a lie, about my father and millions of others, men and women who worked harder than anyone, harder than financiers and politicians, harder than *anybody* if you accept that when you work at an unpleasant job that makes it very hard work indeed.

My mother worked and worked without getting paid at all. She was a plump woman, with a sweet, oval Russian face—a beauty, in fact. She had grown up in Irkutsk, in Siberia. While my father worked *his* hours on the job, she worked all day and all night, managing the family, finding the food, cooking and cleaning, taking the kids to the doctor or the hospital clinic for measles and mumps and whooping cough and tonsillitis and whatever came up. And taking care of family finances. My father had a fourth-grade education and could not read much or do much arithmetic. My mother had gone as far as seventh grade, but her intelligence went far beyond that; she was the brains of the family. And the strength of the family.

Her name was Jenny. Roz and I sat with her in our kitchen one day when she was in her seventies and had her talk about her life, with a tape recorder on the table. She told of her mother's arranged marriage in Irkutsk, of how "they brought a boy home, a Jewish soldier stationed in Irkutsk, and said, This is who you'll marry."

They emigrated to America. Jenny's mother died in her thirties, having given birth to three boys and three girls, and her father—against whom she boiled with indignation all her life—deserted the family. Jenny, the eldest but only a teenager, became the mother of the family, took care of the rest, working in factories, until they grew up and found jobs.

She met Eddie through his sister, who worked in her factory, and it was a passionate marriage all the way. Eddie died at sixty-seven. To the end he was carrying trays of food at weddings and in restaurants, never having made enough money to retire. It was a sudden heart attack, and I got the news in Atlanta, where Roz and I had just moved. I remembered our last meeting, when my father was clearly upset about our little family moving south, so far away, but said nothing except "Good luck. Take care of yourself."

My mother outlived him by many years. She lived by herself, fiercely insisting on her independence, knitting sweaters for everybody, saving her shopping coupons, playing bingo with her friends. But toward the end she suffered a stroke and entered a nursing home.

As a child I was drawn to a framed photograph on the wall, of a delicate-faced little boy with soft brown eyes and a shock of brown hair, and one day my mother told me it was her firstborn, my older brother, who died of spinal meningitis at the age of five. In our tape recording she tells how when he died they'd been in the country for a brief, cheap vacation, and how she and my father held the boy's body on the long train ride back to New York City.

We lived in a succession of tenements, sometimes four rooms, sometimes three. Some winters we lived in a building with central heating. Other times we lived in what was called a cold-water flat— no heat except from the coal cooking stove in the kitchen, no hot water except what we boiled on that same stove.

It was always a battle to pay the bills. I would come home from school in the winter, when the sun set at four, and find the house dark—the electric company had turned off the electricity, and my mother would be sitting there, knitting by candlelight.

There was no refrigerator, but an icebox, for which we would go to the "ice dock" and buy a five- or ten-cent chunk of ice. In the winter a wooden box rested on the sill just outside the window, using nature to keep things cold. There was no shower, but the washtub in the kitchen was our bathtub.

No radio for a long time, until one day my father took me on a long walk through the city to find a second-hand radio, and triumphantly brought it home on his shoulder, me trotting along by his side. No telephone. We could be called to the phone at the candy store down the block, and pay the kid who ran upstairs to get us two pennies or a nickel. Sometimes we hung out near the phone to take the call and race to collect the nickel.

And yes, the roaches. Never absent, wherever we lived. We'd come home and they'd be all over the kitchen table and scatter when we turned on the light. I never got used to them.

I don't remember ever being hungry. The rent might not be paid (we moved often, a step ahead of eviction), no bills might be paid, the grocer might not be paid, but my mother was ingenious at making sure there was always food. Always hot cereal in the morning, always hot soup in the evening, always bread, butter, eggs, milk, noodles and cheese, sour cream, chicken fricassee.

My mother was not shy about using the English language, which she adapted to her purposes. We would hear her telling her friend about the problem she was having with "very close veins," or "a pain in my crutch." She would look in the dairy store for "monster cheese." She would say to my father if he forgot something, "Eddie, try to remember, wreck your brains."

My brothers—Bernie, Jerry, Shelly—and I had lots of fun over the years recalling her ways. She would sign her letters to us, "Your mother, Jenny Zinn." We laughed at those memories even while standing by in the hospital room where she lay in a coma, kept "alive" by a tangle of tubes, her brain already damaged beyond repair. We had signed that terrible order, "Do Not Resuscitate," shortly after which she coughed up her breathing tube and died. She was ninety.

We four boys grew up together—sleeping two or three to a bed, in rooms dark and uninviting. So I spent a lot of time in the street or the schoolyard, playing handball, football, softball, stickball, or taking boxing lessons from a guy in the neighborhood who had made the Golden Gloves and was our version of a celebrity.

In the time I did spend in the house I read. From the time I was eight I was reading whatever books I could find. The very first was one I picked up on the street. The beginning pages were torn out, but that didn't matter. It was *Tarzan and the Jewels of Opar* and from then on I was a fan of Edgar Rice Burroughs, not only his Tarzan books but his other fantasies: *The Chessmen of Mars*, about the way wars were fought by Martians, with warriors, on foot or on horses, playing out the chess moves; *The Earth's Core*, about a strange civilization in the center of the earth.

There were no books in our house. My father had never read a book. My mother read romance magazines. They both read the newspaper. They knew little about politics, except that Franklin Roosevelt was a good man because he helped the poor.

As a boy I read no children's books. My parents did not know about such books, but when I was ten, the *New York Post* offered a set of the complete works of Charles Dickens (of whom they had never heard, of course). By using coupons cut out of the newspaper, they could get a volume every week for a few pennies. They signed up because they knew I loved to read. And so I read Dickens in the order in which we received the books, starting with *David Copperfield*, *Oliver Twist*, *Great Expectations*, *The Pickwick Papers*, *Hard Times*, *A Tale of Two Cities*, and all the rest, until the coupons were exhausted and so was I.

I did not know where Dickens fitted into the history of modern literature because he was all I knew of that literature. I did not know that he was probably the most popular novelist in the English-speaking world (perhaps in any world) in the mid-nineteenth century, or that he was a great actor whose readings of his own work drew mobs of people, or that when he visited the United States in 1842 (he was thirty), landing first in Boston, some of his readers traveled two thousand miles from the Far West to see him.

What I did know was that he aroused in me tumultuous emotions. First, an anger at arbitrary power puffed up with wealth and kept in place by law. But most of all a profound compassion for the poor. I did not see myself as poor in the way Oliver Twist was poor. I didn't recognize that I was so moved by his story because his life touched chords in mine.

How wise Dickens was to make readers feel poverty and cruelty through the fate of children who had not reached the age where the righteous and comfortable classes could accuse them of being responsible for their own misery.

Today, reading pallid, cramped novels about "relationships," I recall Dickens' unashamed rousing of feeling, his uproariously funny characters, his epic settings—cities of hunger and degradation, countries in revolution, the stakes being life and death not just for one family but for thousands.

Dickens is sometimes criticized by literary snobs for sentimentality, melodrama, partisanship, exaggeration. But surely the state of the world makes fictional exaggeration unnecessary and partisanship vital. It was only many years after I read those Dickens novels that I understood his accomplishment.

For my thirteenth birthday, my parents, knowing that I was writing things in notebooks, bought me a rebuilt Underwood typewriter. It came with a practice book for learning the touch system, and soon I was typing book reviews for everything I read and keeping them in my drawer. I never showed them to anyone. It gave me joy and pride just to know that I had read these books and could write about them—on a typewriter.

From the age of fourteen I had after-school and summer jobs, delivering clothes for a dry cleaner, working as a caddy on a golf course in Queens. I also helped out in a succession of candy stores my parents bought in a desperate attempt to make enough money so my father could quit being a waiter. The stores all failed, but my three younger brothers and I had lots of milkshakes and ice cream and candy while they existed.

I remember the last of those candy store situations, and it was typical. The six of us lived above the store in a four-room flat in a dirty old five-story tenement on Bushwick Avenue in Brooklyn. The street was always full of life, especially in spring and summer, when everyone seemed to be outside—old folks sitting on chairs, mothers holding their babies, teenagers playing ball, the older guys "throwing the bull," fooling with girls.

I especially remember that time because I was seventeen and had begun to be interested in world politics.

I was reading books about fascism in Europe. George Seldes' *Sawdust Caesar*, about Mussolini's seizure of power in Italy, fascinated me. I could not get out of my mind the courage of the Socialist deputy Matteotti, who defied Mussolini and was dragged from his home and killed by brown-shirted thugs.

I read something called *The Brown Book of the Nazi Terror*, which described what was happening in Germany under Hitler. It was a drama beyond anything a playwright or novelist could imagine. And now the Nazi war machine was beginning to move into the Rhineland, Austria, Czechoslovakia. The newspapers and radio were full of excitement: Chamberlain meeting Hitler at Munich, the sudden, astonishing nonaggression pact of the two archenemies, Soviet Russia and Nazi Germany. And finally, the invasion of Poland and the start of the Second World War.

The Civil War in Spain, just ended with victory for the Fascist general Franco, seemed the event closest to all of us because several thousand American radicals—Communists, socialists, anarchists—had crossed the Atlantic to fight with the democratic government of Spain. A young fellow who played street football with us—short and thin, the fastest runner in the neighborhood—disappeared. Months later the word came to us: Jerry has gone to Spain to fight against Franco.

There on Bushwick Avenue, among the basketball players and street talkers, were some young Communists, a few years older than me. They had jobs, but after work and on weekends they distributed Marxist literature in the neighborhood and talked politics into the night with whoever was interested.

I was interested. I was reading about what was happening in the world. I argued with the Communist guys. Especially about the Russian invasion of Finland. They insisted it was necessary for the Soviet Union to protect itself against future attack, but to me it was a brutal act of aggression against a tiny country, and none of their carefully worked out justifications persuaded me.

Still, I agreed with them on lots of things. They were ferociously antifascist, indignant as I was about the contrasts of wealth and poverty in America. I admired them—they seemed to know so much about politics, economics, what was happening everywhere in the world. And they were courageous—I had seen them defy the local policeman, who tried to stop them from distributing literature on the street and to break up their knots of discussion. And besides, they were regular guys, good athletes.

One summer day they asked me if I wanted to go with them to "a demonstration" in Times Square that evening. I had never been to such a thing. I made some excuse to my parents, and a little bunch of us took the subway to Times Square.

When we arrived it was just a typical evening in Times Square—the streets crowded, the lights glittering. "Where's the demonstration?" I asked my friend Leon. He was tall, blond, the ideal "Aryan" type, but the son of German Communists who were also nature worshippers and part of a little colony of health-conscious German socialists out in the New Jersey countryside.

"Wait," he said. "Ten o'clock." We continued to stroll.

As the clock on the Times tower struck ten, the scene changed. In the midst of the crowd, banners were unfurled, and people, perhaps a thousand or more, formed into lines carrying banners and signs and chanting slogans about peace and justice and a dozen other causes of the day. It was exciting. And nonthreatening. All these people were keeping to the sidewalks, not blocking traffic, walking in orderly, nonviolent lines through Times Square. My friend and I were walking behind two women carrying a banner, and he said, "Let's relieve them." So we each took an end of the banner. I felt a bit like Charlie Chaplin in *Modern Times*, when he casually picks up a red signal flag and suddenly finds a thousand people marching behind him with raised fists.

We heard the sound of sirens and I thought there must be a fire somewhere, an accident of some kind. But then I heard screams and saw hundreds of policemen, mounted on horses and on foot, charging into the lines of marchers, smashing people with their clubs.

I was astonished, bewildered. This was America, a country where, whatever its faults, people could speak, write, assemble, demonstrate without fear. It was in the Constitution, the Bill of Rights. We were a *democracy*.

As I absorbed this, as my thoughts raced, all in a few seconds, I was spun around by a very large man, who seized my shoulder and hit me very hard. I only saw him as a blur. I didn't know if it was a club or a fist or a blackjack, but I was knocked unconscious.

I awoke in a doorway perhaps a half-hour later. I had no sense of how much time had elapsed, but it was an eerie scene I woke up to. There was no demonstration going on, no policemen in sight. My friend Leon was gone, and Times Square was filled with its usual Saturday night crowd—all as if nothing had happened, as if it were all a dream. But I knew it wasn't a dream; there was a painful lump on the side of my head.

More important, there was a very painful thought in my head: those young Communists on the block were right! The state and its police were not neutral referees in a society of contending interests.

They were on the side of the rich and powerful. Free speech? Try it and the police will be there with their horses, their clubs, their guns, to stop you.

From that moment on, I was no longer a liberal, a believer in the self-correcting character of American democracy. I was a radical, believing that something fundamental was wrong in this country—not just the existence of poverty amidst great wealth, not just the horrible treatment of black people, but something rotten at the root. The situation required not just a new president or new laws, but an uprooting of the old order, the introduction of a new kind of society—cooperative, peaceful, egalitarian.

Perhaps I am exaggerating the importance of that one experience. But I think not. I have come to believe that our lives can be turned in a different direction, our minds adopt a different way of thinking, because of some significant though small event. That belief can be frightening or exhilarating, depending on whether you just contemplate the event or *do* something with it.

The years following that experience in Times Square might be called "my Communist years," but that phrase would be easy to misunderstand because the word "Communist" conjures up Joseph Stalin and the gulags of death and torture, the disappearance of free expression, the atmosphere of fear and trembling created in the Soviet Union, the ugly bureaucracy that lasted seventy years, pretending to be socialism.

None of that was in the minds or intentions of the young working-class people I knew who called themselves Communists. Certainly not in my mind. Little was known about the Soviet Union, except the romantic image, popularized by people like the English theologian Hewlitt Johnson, the Dean of Canterbury. In his book *The Soviet Power*, distributed widely by the Communist movement, he gave idealists disillusioned with capitalism the vision they longed for, of a place where the country belonged to "the people," where everyone had work and free health care, and women had equal opportunities with men, and a hundred different ethnic groups were treated with respect.

The Soviet Union was this romantic blur, far away. What was

close at hand, visible, was that Communists were the leaders in organizing working people all over the country. They were the most daring, risking arrest and beatings to organize auto workers in Detroit, steel workers in Pittsburgh, textile workers in North Carolina, fur and leather workers in New York, longshoremen on the West Coast. They were the first to speak up, more than that, to demonstrate—to chain themselves to factory gates and White House fences—when blacks were lynched in the South, when the "Scottsboro Boys" were being railroaded to prison in Alabama.

My image of "a Communist" was not a Soviet bureaucrat but my friend Leon's father, a cabdriver who came home from work bruised and bloody one day, beaten up by his employer's goons (yes, that word was soon part of my vocabulary) for trying to organize his fellow cabdrivers into a union.

Everyone knew that the Communists were the first antifascists, protesting against Mussolini's invasion of Ethiopia and Hitler's persecution of the Jews. And, most impressive of all, it was the Communists, thousands of them, who volunteered to fight in Spain in the Abraham Lincoln Brigade, to join volunteers from all over the world to defend Madrid and the Spanish people against the army of Francisco Franco, which was given arms and airplanes by Germany and Italy.

Furthermore, some of the best people in the country were connected with the Communist movement in some way, heroes and heroines one could admire. There was Paul Robeson, the fabulous singer-actor-athlete whose magnificent voice could fill Madison Square Garden, crying out against racial injustice, against fascism. And literary figures (weren't Theodore Dreiser and W. E. B. Du Bois Communists?), and talented, socially conscious Hollywood actors and writers and directors (yes, the Hollywood Ten, hauled before a congressional committee, defended by Humphrey Bogart and so many others).

True, in that movement, as in any other, you could see the righteousness leading to dogmatism, the closed circle of ideas impermeable to doubt, an intolerance of dissent by people who were the most persecuted of dissenters. But however imperfect, even repugnant, were particular policies, particular actions, there remained the purity of the ideal, represented in the theories of Karl Marx and the noble visions of many lesser thinkers and writers.

I remember my first reading of *The Communist Manifesto*, which Marx and Engels wrote when they too were young radicals; Marx was thirty, Engels twenty-eight. "The history of all hitherto existing society is the history of class struggle." That was undeniably true, verifiable in any reading of history. Certainly true for the United States, despite all the promises of the Constitution ("We the people of the United States . . ." and "No state shall deny . . . the equal protection of the laws").

The analysis of capitalism by Marx and Engels made sense: capitalism's history of exploitation, its creation of extremes of wealth and poverty, even in the liberal "democracy" of this country. And their socialist vision was not one of dictatorship or bureaucracy but of a free society. Their "dictatorship of the proletariat" was to be a transitional phase, the goal a classless society of true democracy, true freedom. A rational, just economic system would allow a short work day and leave everyone freedom and time to do as they liked—to write poetry, to be in nature, to play sports, to be truly human. Nationalism would be a thing of the past. People all over the world, of whatever race, of whatever continent, would live in peace and cooperation.

In my teenage reading, those ideas were kept alive by some of the finest writers in America. I read Upton Sinclair's *The Jungle*; work in the Chicago stockyards was the epitome of capitalist exploitation, and the vision of a new society in the last pages of the book is thrilling. John Steinbeck's *The Grapes of Wrath* was an eloquent cry against the conditions of life wherein the poor were expendable and any attempt on their part to change their lives was met with police clubs.

When I was eighteen, unemployed and my family desperate for help, I took a much-publicized Civil Service examination for a job in the Brooklyn Navy Yard. Thirty thousand young men (women applicants were unthinkable) took the exam, competing for a few hundred jobs. It was 1940, and New Deal programs had relieved but not ended the Depression. When the results were announced, four hundred of the applicants had gotten a score of 100 percent on the exam and would get jobs. I was one of them.

For me and my family it was a triumph. My salary would be $14.40 for a forty-hour week. I could give the family $10 a week and have the rest for lunch and spending money.

It was also an introduction into the world of heavy industry. I was to be an apprentice shipfitter for the next three years. I would work out on "the ways," a vast inclined surface at the edge of the harbor on which a battleship, the USS *Iowa*, was to be built. (Many years later, in the 1980s, I was called to be a witness at the Staten Island trial of pacifists who had demonstrated against the placement of nuclear weapons on a battleship docked there—the USS *Iowa*.)

I had no idea of the dimensions of a battleship. Stood on end, it would have been almost as tall as the Empire State Building. The keel had just been laid, and our job—thousands of us—was to put together the steel body and inner framework of the ship. It was hard, dirty, malodorous work. The smell caused by cutting galvanized steel with an acetylene torch is indescribable—only years later did we learn that the zinc released in such burning also causes cancer.

In the winter, icy blasts blew from the sea, and we wore thick gloves and helmets, and got occasional relief around the little fires used by the riveters. They heated their rivets in these fires until the rivets were glowing globules which they then pulled from the fire and pounded into the steel plates of the hull with huge hammers driven by compressed air. The sound was deafening.

In the summer, we sweated under our overalls and in our steel-tipped boots, and swallowed salt pills to prevent heat exhaustion. We did a lot of crawling around inside the tiny steel compartments of the "inner bottom," where smells and sounds were magnified a hundred times. We measured and hammered, and cut and welded, using the service of "burners" and "chippers."

No women workers. The skilled jobs were held by white men, who were organized in A. F. of L. craft unions known to be inhospitable to blacks. The few blacks in the shipyard had the toughest, most physically demanding jobs, like riveting.

What made the job bearable was the steady pay and the accompanying dignity of being a workingman, bringing home money like my father. There was also the pride that we were doing something for the war effort. But most important for me was that I found a small group of friends, fellow apprentices—some of them shipfitters like myself, others shipwrights, machinists, pipefitters, sheetmetal workers—who were young radicals, determined to do something to change the world. No less.

We were excluded from the craft unions of the skilled workers, so we decided to organize the apprentices into a union, an association. We would act together to improve our working conditions, raise our pay, and create a camaraderie during and after working hours to add some fun to our workaday lives.

This we did, successfully, with three hundred young workers, and for me it was an introduction to actual participation in a labor movement. We were organizing a union and doing what working people had done through the centuries, creating little spaces of culture and friendship to make up for the dreariness of the work itself.

Four of us who were elected as officers of the Apprentice Association became special friends. We met one evening a week to read books on politics and economics and socialism, and talk about world affairs. These were years when some fellows our age were in college, but we felt we were getting a good education.

Still, I was glad to leave the shipyard and join the Air Force. And it was while flying combat missions in Europe that I began a sharp turn in my political thinking, away from the romanticization of the Soviet Union that enveloped many radicals (and others, too), especially in the atmosphere of World War II and the stunning successes of the Red Army against the Nazi invaders.

The reason for this turn was my encounter, which I described earlier, with an aerial gunner on another crew who questioned whether the aims of the Allies—England, France, the United States, the Soviet Union—were really antifascist and democratic.

One book he gave me shook forever ideas I had held for years. This was *The Yogi and the Commissar*, by Arthur Koestler. Koestler had been a Communist, had fought in Spain, but he had become convinced—and his factual evidence was powerful, his logic unshakable—that the Soviet Union, with its claim to be a socialist state, was a fraud. (After the war I read *The God That Failed*, in which writers whose integrity and dedication to justice I could not question—Richard Wright, André Gide, Ignazio Silone, and Koestler, too—describe their loss of faith in the Communist movement and the Soviet Union.)

But disillusionment with the Soviet Union did not diminish my belief in socialism, any more than disillusionment with the United States government lessened my belief in democracy. It certainly did not affect my consciousness of *class*, of the difference in the way rich and poor lived in the United States, of the failure of the society to provide the most basic biological necessities—food, housing, health care—to tens of millions of people.

Oddly enough, when I became a second lieutenant in the Army Air Corps I got a taste of what life was like for the privileged classes—for now I had better clothes, better food, more money, higher status than I had in civilian life.

After the war, with a few hundred dollars in mustering-out money, and my uniform and medals packed away, I rejoined Roz. We were a young, happy married couple. But we could find no other place to live but a rat-infested basement apartment in Bedford-Stuyvesant ("rat-infested" is not a figure of speech—there was that day I walked into the bathroom and saw a large rat scurry up the water pipe back into the ceiling).

I was back in the working class, but needing a job. I tried going back to the Brooklyn Navy Yard, but it was hateful work with none of the compensating features of that earlier time. I worked as a waiter, as a ditch-digger, as a brewery worker, and collected unemployment insurance in between jobs. (I can understand very well the feeling of veterans of the Vietnam War, who were *important* when soldiers, coming back home with no jobs, no prospects, and without the glow that surrounded the veterans of World War II—

a diminishing of their selves.) In the meantime, our daughter, Myla, was born.

At the age of twenty-seven, with a second child on the way, I began college as a freshman at New York University, under the G.I. Bill of Rights. That gave me four years of free college education and $120 a month, so that with Roz working part-time, with Myla and Jeff in nursery, with me working a night shift after school, we could survive.

Whenever I hear that the government *must not* get involved in helping people, that this must be left to "private enterprise," I think of the G.I. Bill and its marvelous nonbureaucratic efficiency. There are certain necessities—housing, medical care, education—about which private enterprise gives not a hoot (supplying these to the poor is not profitable, and private enterprise won't act without *profit*).

Starting college coincided with a change in our lives: moving out of our miserable basement rooms into a low-income housing project in downtown Manhattan, on the East River. Four rooms, utilities included in the rent, no rats, no cockroaches, a few trees and a playground downstairs, a park along the river. We were happy.

While going to N.Y.U. and Columbia I worked the four-to-twelve shift in the basement of a Manhattan warehouse, loading heavy cartons of clothing onto trailer trucks which would carry them to cities all over the country.

We were an odd crew, we warehouse loaders—a black man, a Honduran immigrant, two men somewhat retarded mentally, another veteran of the war (married, with children, he sold his blood to supplement his small pay check). With us for a while was a young man named Jeff Lawson whose father was John Howard Lawson, a Hollywood writer, one of the Hollywood Ten. There was another young fellow, a Columbia College student who was named after his grandfather, the socialist labor leader Daniel DeLeon. (I encountered him many years later; he was in a bad way mentally, and then I got word that he had laid down under his car in the garage and breathed in enough carbon monoxide to kill himself.)

We were all members of the union (District 65), which had a reputation of being "left-wing." But we, the truck-loaders, were more left than the union, which seemed hesitant to interfere with the loading operation of this warehouse.

We were angry about our working conditions, having to load outside on the sidewalk in bad weather with no rain or snow gear available to us. We kept asking the company for gear, with no results. One night, late, the rain began pelting down. We stopped work, said we would not continue unless we had a binding promise of rain gear.

The supervisor was beside himself. That truck had to get out that night to meet the schedule, he told us. He had no authority to promise anything. We said, "Tough shit. We're not getting drenched for the damned schedule." He got on the phone, nervously called a company executive at his home, interrupting a dinner party. He came back from the phone. "Okay, you'll get your gear." The next workday we arrived at the warehouse and found a line of shiny new raincoats and rainhats.

That was my world for the first thirty-three years of my life—the world of unemployment and bad employment, of me and my wife leaving our two- and three-year-olds in the care of others while we went to school or to work, living most of that time in cramped and unpleasant places, hesitating to call the doctor when the children were sick because we couldn't afford to pay him, finally taking the children to hospital clinics where interns could take care of them. This is the way a large part of the population lives, even in this, the richest country in the world. And when, armed with the proper degrees, I began to move out of that world, becoming a college professor, I never forgot that. I never stopped being class-conscious.

I note how our political leaders step gingerly around such expressions, how it seems the worst accusation one politician can make about another is that "he appeals to class hostility . . . he is setting class against class." Well, class has been set against class in the realities of life for a very long time, and the words will disappear only when the realities of inequity disappear.

It would be foolish for me to claim that class consciousness was simply the result of growing up poor and living the life of a poor kid and then the life of a hard-pressed young husband and father. I've met many people with similar backgrounds who developed a very different set of ideas about society, and many others, whose early lives were much different from mine but whose world-view is similar.

When I was chair of the history department at Spelman and had the power (even a *little power* can make people heady!) to actually hire one or two people, I invited Staughton Lynd, a brilliant young historian, graduate of Harvard and Columbia, to join the Spelman faculty. (We were introduced at a historians' meeting in New York, where Staughton expressed a desire to teach at a black college.)

The summer before Staughton Lynd came south, we met in New England and decided to climb a New Hampshire mountain (Mt. Monadnock) together and get acquainted. My two children, Myla and Jeff, came with us. They were thirteen and eleven. When we reached the summit, tired and hungry, we found the remains of a pack of cigarettes, and the four of us—all nonsmokers, it is fair to say—sat down cross-legged and puffed silently, pretending we were characters in *Treasure of the Sierra Madre*.

That mountain-climbing conversation was illuminating. Staughton came from a background completely different from mine. His parents were quite famous professors at Columbia and Sarah Lawrence, Robert and Helen Lynd, authors of the sociological classic *Middletown*. Staughton had been raised in comfortable circumstances, had gone to Harvard and Columbia. And yet, as we went back and forth on every political issue under the sun—— race, class, war, violence, nationalism, justice, fascism, capitalism, socialism, and more—it was clear that our social philosophies, our values, were extraordinarily similar.

In the light of such experiences, traditional dogmatic "class analysis" cannot remain intact. But as dogma disintegrates, hope appears. Because it seems that human beings, whatever their backgrounds, are more open than we think, that their behaviour cannot be confidently predicted from their past, that we are all creatures vulnerable to new thoughts, new attitudes.

And while such vulnerability creates all sorts of possibilities, both good and bad, its very existence is exciting. It means that no human being should be written off, no change in thinking deemed impossible.

A Yellow
Rubber Chicken:
Battles At
Boston University

From the start, my teaching was infused with my own history. I would try to be fair to other points of view, but I wanted more than "objectivity"; I wanted students to leave my classes not just better informed, but more prepared to relinquish the safety of silence, more prepared to speak up, to act against injustice wherever they saw it. This, of course, was a recipe for trouble.

Boston University's Department of Political Science, knowing I was no longer at Spelman (I was in Boston, writing two books on the South and the movement) offered me a job, to start in the fall of 1964. I accepted. They did not seem to be interested in the circumstances of my leaving Spelman. They had heard me give a lecture at B.U. several years earlier, they knew I had written a book which was given a prize by the American Historical Association (*La-Guardia in Congress*), and articles on the South for *Harper's*, the *Nation*, and the *New Republic*. So I seemed to them a likely prospect.

But the beginning of my teaching at Boston University coincided almost exactly with the steep escalation of the United States' war in

Vietnam, after the hazy incident in the Gulf of Tonkin. I became involved immediately in the protests against the war: rallies, teach-ins, demonstrations, articles—one of these, for the *Nation*, arguing the case for withdrawal from Vietnam.

When I was hired, I was promised tenure after a year, which is a fairly strong guarantee of lifetime employment. But following that first year I was still without a tenure contract. A secretarial error, I was told. Another year passed (in which my antiwar activity increased) and another excuse was given.

Finally, in early 1967, the Department of Political Science held a meeting to vote on my tenure. There were a few professors opposed, saying flatly that my actions against the war were embarrassing to the university. On the other hand, student evaluations of my teaching were enthusiastic, and my fifth book was being published that spring. The department voted for tenure.

Approval came soon from the dean and the president. (This was four years before John Silber became president of the university.) All that remained was a vote of the Board of Trustees.

That spring of 1967, some students came to my office saying that the trustees were going to have their annual meeting, to coincide with a Founders Day dinner, and that the guest speaker would be Dean Rusk, secretary of state, in a splendid affair at the Sheraton Boston Hotel. Rusk was one of the strategists of the Vietnam War, and the students were going to organize a demonstration in front of the hotel. They wanted me to be one of the speakers.

I hesitated as I thought of my tenure decision in the hands of the trustees. But I could hardly say no—hadn't I always maintained that risking your job is a price you pay if you want to be a free person? I must confess that my courage was not absolute; I envisioned that I would be one of many speakers and perhaps not be noticed.

When the evening of the big event came, I made my way to the Sheraton Boston and joined several hundred demonstrators circling in front of the hotel. Soon one of the organizers came to escort me to the microphone, which was set up near the hotel entrance. I looked around. "Where are the other speakers?" I asked. He looked puzzled. "There are no other speakers."

And so I held forth to the crowd assembled in front of the hotel, talking about the war and why the United States did not belong in Vietnam. As I spoke, limousines drew up, one by one, and tuxedoed guests, including Dean Rusk, the trustees, and others, stepped out, stopped for a moment to take in the scene, and went into the hotel.

A few days later I received a letter from the Office of the President. As I opened it, I thought of that other letter of 1963 from the office of another president. But this one said, "Dear Professor Zinn, I am happy to inform you that you have been awarded tenure by a meeting of the Board of Trustees on the afternoon of . . ." So the trustees had voted me tenure in the afternoon, then arrived in the evening for the Founders Day dinner to find their newly tenured faculty member denouncing their honored guest.

Without that lucky winning of tenure, John Silber's arrival as president of Boston University would have ended my job. He had been a professor of philosophy and a dean at the University of Texas. He was fast talking and fast thinking and two philosophers on the B.U. presidential search committee had recommended him on the basis of what I believe is a common fallacy among intellectuals, that to say someone is "bright," even "brilliant," as was said of Silber, is equivalent to saying someone is *good*.

Silber and I clashed almost immediately. What seemed to infuriate him was that I dared to criticize him publicly and unsparingly. (Yes, as the president of Spelman had said, I was insubordinate.)

One of the first things President Silber did upon taking office was to invite the U.S. Marines to the university to recruit students for the Marine Corps. This was in the spring of 1972, with the war in Vietnam still going on. Antiwar students organized a demonstration, sitting on the steps of the building where the recruiters were ensconced. It was nonviolent, but obstructive, no doubt, making it not impossible but difficult for students to meet with the recruiter.

I was not in that demonstration, but home in bed with a bad viral infection. Someone phoned me with the news: Silber had called the police, and was there on the scene with a bullhorn, acting like a general in a military operation as the police moved in, using police dogs and clubs, to arrest the demonstrators.

The next day, the official administration newspaper carried the headline "Disruptive Students Must Be Taught Respect for Law, Says Dr. Silber."

Still in bed, I wrote an article about the incident for a Boston newspaper, and it was widely reprinted on campus. I wanted to engage Silber on the history of the U.S. Marines, the philosophy of civil disobedience, and the concept of an "open university," a principle he claimed he was upholding by inviting the Marines to recruit.

"It is true," I wrote, "that one crucial function of the schools is training people to take the jobs that society has to offer. . . . But the much more important function of organized education is to teach the new generation that rule without which the leaders could not possibly carry on wars, ravage the country's wealth, keep down rebels and dissenters—the rule of obedience to legal authority. And no one can do that more skillfully, more convincingly than the professional intellectual. A philosopher turned university president is best of all. If his arguments don't work on the students—who sometimes prefer to look at the world around them than to read Kant—then he can call in the police, and after that momentary interruption (the billy club serving as exclamation point to the rational argument) the discussion can continue, in a more subdued atmosphere."

In what seemed to me a peculiar interpretation, Silber pointed to the example of Martin Luther King, Jr., in arguing that students should give themselves up to arrest for what they had done. This led me to write: "How odd that a man whose own behavior that day more closely resembled that of Birmingham's Bull Connor—replete with police dogs, hidden photographers, and club-wielding police—should invoke the name of Martin Luther King, who would have been there on the steps with the students."

Silber declared his educational philosophy in 1976 on the op-ed page of the *New York Times*. He wrote: "As Jefferson recognized, there is a natural aristocracy among men. The grounds of this are virtue and talent. . . . Democracy freed from a counterfeit and ultimately destructive egalitarianism provides a society in which the wisest, the best, and the most dedicated assume positions of leadership. . . . As long as intelligence is better than stupidity, knowledge than ignorance, and virtue than vice, no university can be run except on an elitist basis." On another occasion, Silber said, "The more democratic a university is, the lousier it is."

His supreme confidence in his own intelligence, knowledge, and virtue led him to be arrogant with faculty, contemptuous of students, and to behave more and more like a petty dictator in running the university.

When his five-year contract expired in 1976, there was a campuswide movement involving students, faculty, and deans, urging that he not be kept on. The faculty voted overwhelmingly that he should not be rehired, and fifteen of the sixteen deans concurred.

The decision, however, rested with the Board of Trustees. When a committee of the trustees recommended that his contract should not be renewed, Silber, ever the fighter, insisted on appearing before the board, and persuaded them to keep him on. After that close call, he set about to ensure his position. The deans who had called for his departure did not stay long. One by one they disappeared. A new chairman of the Board of Trustees took over—Arthur Metcalf, an industrialist and militarist (he wrote a column for a right-wing journal on military strategy) and a close friend of Silber's. (Soon after, Silber acquired stock in Metcalf's corporation, which he later sold for over a million dollars.)

After twenty years in the presidency, Silber pointed to how much money he had added to the university's endowment, and this was true, although it was also true that he had added a comparable amount to the university's debt. He was proud of the fact that he brought some distinguished people to the faculty. Indeed he did, but it was also a fact that many fine teachers left Boston University because they could not stand the atmosphere created by his administration.

His claim was that he had turned a mediocre institution into a "world-class university." To many of us, this was a bit like Mussolini trampling on civil liberties while boasting that he had made Italy into an important power, had brought order, had made the trains run on time.

Shortly after the trustees renewed his contract in 1976, Silber established censorship of student publications, requiring them to have faculty advisers who would have approval over what was printed. I was an adviser to one student newspaper, *The Exposure*, whose bold criticism of the administration undoubtedly led to the censorship policy. When I refused to act as censor the paper was denied funds to operate, and when student organizations voted to allocate money for it, the administration blocked the funding.

In 1978, the radical attorney William Kunstler was invited to speak at the B.U. Law School. In the course of his remarks he made a joking and unflattering remark about President Silber. The executive director of the Boston University radio station, who had planned to air the speech, was ordered to delete the remark from the tape. He refused, and, as he told me later, an administration official took him outside the building and presented him with a choice: resign or be fired. He resigned.

The Civil Liberties Union of Massachusetts, in its report of 1979, said it had "never, in memory, received such a large and sustained volume of complaints about a single . . . institution" as about Boston University, and that its investigation had led it to believe "that B.U. has violated fundamental principles of civil liberties and academic freedom."

Faculty members who did not have tenure became fearful of voicing criticism of the president. Those who spoke out, even if faculty committees on four different levels voted for them, faced the loss of their jobs. Silber had absolute power to overrule all faculty decisions on tenure, and used it.

Boston University, under Silber, became notorious throughout academia. University police, sometimes overtly, sometimes surreptitiously, took photos of students and faculty who participated in demonstrations. I remember one such picket line, with faculty and students walking peacefully outside the building where the trustees were meeting, carrying signs against apartheid in South Africa. A university security guard, with a dean standing nearby, put his camera right up to our faces, one by one, to take his photos.

A student who distributed leaflets in the hall outside another trustees' meeting was suspended for a semester. Another student, who distributed leaflets outside the stadium where a commencement was taking place, was ordered to leave or be arrested.

A graduating honors student about to go to law school, Maureen Judge, being interviewed for a university brochure, was asked to name "my two most inspiring and enjoyable professors." She named me as one of them, and then was told the interview would not be published unless she deleted my name. She refused.

One day a student named Yosef Abramowitz, active in Zionist affairs and also in the campaign to get B.U. to divest itself of its South African stocks, came to my office to tell me a disturbing story. He had hung a sign from his dormitory window with one word on it: "Divest." University workers were ordered to remove the sign. Twice more he put it up, twice more it was removed. He received a letter from the administration: he would be evicted from his room if he insisted on replacing the sign.

From my office, we called the Civil Liberties Union. They contacted a young lawyer in the area to ask if he would handle the case—it was an opportunity to test a new Massachusetts law on civil rights. The lawyer responded, "I'll be happy to take the case. I just graduated from the B.U. Law School."

I went to court to listen. The university's lawyer insisted that the word "divest" was not the problem. The issue was an aesthetic one: the sign, he said, disturbed the beauty of the neighborhood. To anyone who knew that neighborhood, or the architecture of Boston University, this was a hilarious statement.

Abramowitz's lawyer put on the witness stand student after student who testified about the things they had hung from their windows (for one, a yellow rubber chicken) without any complaint from the administration.

The judge made his decision: B.U. must stop interfering with Abramowitz's right of free speech.

As word spread about the strange events at Boston University, journalists trying to uncover what was going on reported again and again that faculty members were afraid to go on public record as being critical of the administration. A reporter for the *New York Times Magazine* wrote, "Most of the people—B.U. students and faculty, former faculty, former trustees—interviewed for this article, even those with nothing critical to say, wished to remain anonymous for fear of reprisals."

Meanwhile, Silber was raising his own salary in huge jumps, so that soon, at $275,000 a year, he made more than the presidents of Harvard, Yale, Princeton, or M.I.T. Furthermore, he was getting special deals from the Board of Trustees: real estate sold to him at below the market price for his use as rental property, loans at little or no interest, a generous bonus package on top of his salary. As university president he had become a millionaire, not a customary thing in the academic world.

When questioned about the money spent to lavishly furnish his rent-free house, Silber would respond, "Do you want your president to live in a pup tent on the Charles River?"

His employees, on the other hand, had difficulty getting raises in their wages or their benefits. In self-defense they organized into unions: the faculty, the secretaries and staff, the librarians. And in 1979, with various grievances not met, all of these groups, at different times, went out on strike. For the faculty, the provocation was the university reneging on a contract at first agreed to by its negotiating committee.

I was one of the co-chairs of the strike committee of the faculty union (officially called, in the cautious language of college professors, the Postponement Committee). My job was to organize the picket lines at the entrance to every university building, to establish a rotation system among the hundreds of picketers. The faculty was admirable in its tenacity, showing up day after day, from early morning to evening, to walk the picket lines.

Some students complained about the canceled classes, but many came to our support. The normal functioning of the university became impossible. The College of Liberal Arts and a number of other schools were virtually closed down.

After nine days of picketing, endless meetings, strategy sessions, the university gave in. But Silber hated to acknowledge defeat. In a telegram sent to the trustees just before the settlement, he urged that in no way should it be conceded that it was the strike which brought about the university's acceptance of the contract with the union.

In the meantime, however, the secretaries had gone out on strike, too, and we all walked the picket lines together, a rare event in the academic world. Some of us in the faculty union tried to get our colleagues to refuse to go back to work until the administration agreed to a contract with the secretaries, but we failed to persuade. Our contract was signed, and teachers returned to their classes, with the secretaries still walking the picket line.

A number of us refused to cross those picket lines and held our classes out of doors. I met my class of about two hundred students on Commonwealth Avenue, one of the main Boston thorough-fares, in front of the building where we normally met. I rented a loudspeaker system and explained to the class why we were not going inside. We had a lively discussion about the reasons for the strike and how it connected with the subject of our course, "Law and Justice in America."

In the midst of our sidewalk class, the dean of the College of Liberal Arts showed up and handed me a circular from the administration: faculty were expected to meet their classes in their regular places or be considered in violation of their contracts.

A few days later, five faculty who had refused to cross the picket lines were charged with violation of the union contract, which prohibited "sympathy strikes." The article under which we were charged contained a provision which could lead to our being fired, though we all had tenure. In addition to me, there was my friend and colleague in the political science department, Murray Levin, one of the most popular lecturers in the university; Fritz Ringer, a distinguished historian; Andrew Dibner, a much-respected member of the psychology department; and Caryl Rivers, a nationally known columnist and novelist who taught journalism.

Ours soon became "the case of the B.U. Five." We had the help of the faculty union attorney and several outside lawyers. A Nobel

Prize laureate at M.I.T., Dr. Salvadore Luria, organized a defense committee and circulated support petitions to faculty members all over the country. A group of academics in France sent a letter of protest to the Silber administration. The *Boston Globe* and other newspapers wrote editorials accusing the university of violating academic freedom.

A group of distinguished women writers—Grace Paley, Marilyn French, Marge Piercy, Denise Levertov—did readings for an overflow audience at the Arlington Street Church, to raise money for our defense.

The noise around the case must have become too much for John Silber. He backed down. The charges against us were dropped.

Faculty with tenure cannot easily be fired, but they can be punished for dissidence in other ways. When Murray Levin and I were recommended for raises by our department, Silber overturned them, year after year. One of the leaders of the union, Freda Rebelsky, an award-winning teacher and nationally known psychologist, was punished in the same way. Arnold Offner, a historian who had won an award for distinguished teaching, was denied a raise because a right-wing faculty member, a friend of Silber's, objected to something he said in class about American foreign policy.

Silber vetoed raises for me again and again. But our faculty contract had a procedure for appeal to an arbitration committee. In the early 1980s, when Silber once again overruled a department recommendation, the arbitration group went over the evidence (that year, my book *A People's History of the United States* was nominated for an American Book Award) and gave me my raise.

What seemed to anger Silber most was that every semester four hundred or more students would sign up for my lecture course: in the fall, "Law and Justice in America," in the spring, "Introduction to Political Theory." He refused to allot money for a teaching assistant, although classes with a hundred students would routinely have one or two assistants. He let it be known that I could get a teaching assistant if I limited enrollment in my classes to sixty students.

He knew that my classes discussed the most controversial social issues: freedom of expression, the race question, military intervention abroad, economic justice, socialism, capitalism, anarchism. On these issues, Silber and I had very different views. He was an admirer of the military, and apparently believed in supporting any government, whatever its record on human rights, so long as it was anti-Communist. (El Salvador's, for instance, even while that government was collaborating with death squads and terrorism.) He was extremely intolerant of homosexuality and not very enthusiastic about heterosexuality (he instituted a rule forbidding overnight guests of the opposite sex in dorms).

Speaking to a gathering of university presidents on the West Coast, Silber talked darkly about those teachers who "poison the well of academe." His two chief examples: Noam Chomsky and Howard Zinn.

In the fall of 1979, after all the strikes, the faculty began circulating a petition to request the trustees to dismiss Silber. A special assembly of the university faculty was called to vote on the issue. The day before that assembly I was sitting in my office with a student when a colleague who taught in the School of Education walked in. He said that he had just come from a faculty meeting at his school, where Silber had appealed to the faculty to vote down the petition for his removal. The backers of this petition, Silber said, were longtime troublemakers. Even before he'd became president, he said, Howard Zinn had tried to set fire to the president's office.

"You're not serious," I said.

"Oh, yes. He accused you of arson. We all sat there, bewildered. Do you have any idea what he was talking about?"

"No."

The student sitting in the office was interested. She was a graduate student in journalism. She said she would look into this.

Next morning the *Boston Globe* carried a story, prominently displayed, with photos of both Silber and me, and a headline: "Silber Accuses Zinn of Arson." The byline was that of the student who had been in my office. She verified that Silber had made such a statement to the School of Education, but also wrote that she had checked with the fire department. Indeed, there once had been a fire reported in the president's office, before Silber's time, but there was never any indication of whether it was accidental or deliberate and no one had ever been accused.

I began to get phone calls from lawyer friends. This is, they said, a textbook case of defamation, of libel. A terrific opportunity to sue Silber for all he's worth (now a fortune). I wouldn't hear of it. I was not going to get involved in a lawsuit—whatever the prize— that would then dominate my life for years.

That afternoon the faculty assembled for its special meeting. Silber presided. Since the main business was the petition calling for his removal, some thought he would turn the chair over to someone else. But Silber was not one to do that. It was said of Theodore Roosevelt that he had such an ego he wanted to preside over his own funeral; Silber was going to take charge of this meeting.

The hall filled and filled—clearly the largest turnout of faculty anyone could remember. Then Silber took the microphone: "Before the meeting officially begins, I want to apologize to Professor Howard Zinn." There was a buzz of astonishment—no one could imagine Silber ever apologizing to anyone for anything. What I suspected was that his lawyer friends had advised him to do so to minimize what might be a costly and losing lawsuit for defamation of character.

The hall became very quiet as Silber gave his explanation. When he became president he'd been shown slides of the history of activism at B.U. One of them showed an occupation of the president's office, in protest against police brutality on campus, and it showed me as part of the sit-in. Another slide showed a fire at the president's office. They were two separate events, but, Silber explained, he "conflated the two incidents."

The meeting began. Silber's supporters, mostly administrators and department heads, spoke to oppose the resolution. In defense of Silber, one department head rose to quote an American president speaking of a Caribbean dictator: "He may be a son-of-a-bitch. But he's *our* son-of-a-bitch."

Silber's faculty opponents rose to give evidence of financial mis-
management, of how Silber had preempted all important decisions,
disregarded faculty opinion, inhibited freedom of expression,
abused the rights of employees, and created conditions which
blighted teaching and learning.

The vote was taken. It was 457–215 in favor of calling on the
trustees to oust Silber. By now, Silber and Metcalf had tight control
of the board. The trustees rejected the faculty resolution.

Not long after this, a woman in the English department named
Julia Prewitt Brown came up for tenure. She was hopeful; she had
written a much-praised book on novelist Jane Austen. However,
she also had picketed in front of Silber's office during the strike.
Her department voted for her unanimously. Two more faculty
committees voted for her unanimously. When Silber's provost then
turned her down for tenure, an outside committee of three scholars
was called in. They voted in her favor. That added up to forty-two
of her peers urging that she get tenure. But John Silber said no.

Julia Brown was a fighter. As she told me, at one time her father
had been an amateur boxer back in St. Louis, and she'd been a fight
fan from the time she was a girl. She admired fighters (Sugar Ray
Leonard was one) who fought to the end, against whatever odds.
She would not be bullied. She was the mother of three young children, but she would take all her money, sell her condominium in
Boston, hire a lawyer, and sue Silber and B.U.

Her lawyer was Dahlia Rudavsky, also a young mother, who had
been an attorney for the faculty union during and after the strike.
Rudavsky drew up a double charge: political discrimination and
sexual discrimination.

There was a history of Silber mistreating women faculty. Women
were much less likely to get tenure than men, and women whose
political views Silber disliked were especially vulnerable. Two
women in the philosophy department, each exceptional in her own
way, both voted tenure by their departments, were turned down by
Silber, as was a woman in the sociology department who had been
a strong supporter of the strike. Tenure for a woman in the eco-

nomics department, a white South African who was outspoken in her disagreements with Silber about South Africa, was approved by her department, then vetoed by the president's office.

Much of the evidence in the trial centered on the importance of Julia Brown's book on Jane Austen. Silber expressed disdain for Jane Austen as a "lightweight" among novelists, but in the trial admitted he had not read Julia Brown's book. He did not deny that he had called the English department "a damned matriarchy."

The jury quickly came to a conclusion. Boston University and John Silber were guilty of sex discrimination. Julia Brown was awarded $200,000. The judge, in an extraordinary decision (courts customarily stay out of tenure disputes), ordered B.U. to grant her tenure. It had taken six years of persistence on her part, but in the end, like her hero Sugar Ray Leonard outlasting Marvin Hagler for the middleweight championship, she won.

For so many of us who worked at Boston University, it was often discouraging to see how a tyrannical president could hold on to power for so long. But the administration, though it had its admirers, never won the affection of the campus community. And it never succeeded in beating down those students and faculty who were determined to speak their minds, to honor the idea that a university should provide a free and humane atmosphere for humane learning.

The Possibility
of Hope

I have tried hard to match my friends in their pessimism about the world (is it just *my* friends?), but I keep encountering people who, in spite of all the evidence of terrible things happening everywhere, give me hope. Especially young people, in whom the future rests.

I think of my students.

Not just the women of Spelman, who leapt over a hundred years of national disgrace to become part of the civil rights movement.

Not just the fellow in Alice Walker's poem "Once," who acted out the spirit of a new generation:

> It is true—
> I've always loved
> the daring
>   ones
> Like the black young
> man
> Who tried
> to crash
> All barriers

at once,
   wanted to
swim
At a white
beach (in Alabama)
Nude.

I think also of my students at Boston University and of young people all over the country who, anguished about the war in Vietnam, resisted in some way, facing police clubs and arrests. And brave high school students like Mary Beth Tinker and her classmates in Des Moines, Iowa, who insisted on wearing black armbands to protest the war and when suspended from school took their case to the Supreme Court and won.

Of course, some would say, that was the *sixties*.

But even in the seventies and eighties, when there was widespread head-shaking over the "apathy" of the student generation, an impressive number of students continued to act.

I think of the determined little group at B.U. (most of them had never done anything like this, but they were emulating similar groups at a hundred schools around the country) who set up a "shantytown" on campus to represent apartheid in South Africa. The police tore it down, but the students refused to move and were arrested.

In South Africa in the summer of 1982 I had visited Crossroads, a real shantytown outside of Capetown, where thousands of blacks occupied places that looked like chicken coops, or were jammed together in huge tents, sleeping in shifts, six hundred of them sharing one faucet of running water. I was impressed that young Americans who had not seen that with their own eyes, had only read about it or seen photos, would be so moved to step out of their comfortable lives and act.

It went beyond the obviously political issues. Young women were becoming more involved in demanding sexual equality, freedom of choice for abortion, control of their own bodies. Gays and lesbians were speaking out, gradually wearing away the public's longtime prejudices.

Beyond those activists, however, there was a much larger population of students who had no contact with any movement, yet had deep feelings about injustice.

Students kept journals in my courses, where they commented on the issues discussed in class and on the books they had read. They were asked to speak personally, to make connections between what they read and their own lives, their own thoughts. This was in the mid-eighties, supposedly a bad time for social consciousness among students.

A young woman wrote: "After reading Richard Wright's *Black Boy*, I cried for Mr. Wright, for the atrocities that he endured. . . . I cried for all blacks, for the unfair treatment they have continued to receive because they are black. And I cried for myself, because I realized that society has instilled some prejudice in me which I cannot get rid of."

A young man: "Two summers ago I worked at the General Motors plant in Framingham. . . . I learned a great deal in that one summer about what life is to many people. The usual scenario goes something like this: A young kid out of high school is 'lucky' enough to land a job at G.M. . . . Soon he realizes that working at G.M. sucks. The work sucks, the management sucks, and the union isn't even there half the time. . . . So the youngster thinks about his future: 'I hate this place and would love to leave, but I've already got five years under my belt. In only 25 years I can retire with a full pension. And so he decides to stay. Whoosh!!! And his life is gone."

A young woman studying in the school of communications: "I'm photostating logos at work. Logos for television sets. 'Sony. The One and Only.'—'Toshiba, In Touch With Tomorrow'—'Panasonic. Just Slightly Ahead of Our Time.' . . . Why am I surrounded by such nothingness that pretends to be something? My major is advertising. How can I work week after week creating nothingness? . . . Today in the library . . . I spent three hours looking through books on Vietnam. I need to know more. . . . More and more I find myself wondering if I could become a schoolteacher. Somehow I will tell people what I have learned. Show them where to find things out. This will be my war."

A young man from Dorchester (a working-class neighborhood in Boston which led the nation in the proportion of men who died in Vietnam) who worked in the library to help pay his tuition: "America to me is a society, a culture. America is my home; if someone were to rob that *culture* from me, then perhaps there would be reason to resist. I will not die, however, to defend the honor of the *government*."

A young woman in the R.O.T.C. program, after seeing the documentary film *Hearts and Minds*: "I thought I was doing pretty well 'keeping my cool' until I saw the American soldier shoot the Vietnamese. Then I lost it. And then there was a soldier dragging a mutilated dead body, and another kicking a live one. I watched the student next to me dab his eyes and felt glad someone else was just as upset. . . . General Westmoreland said 'Orientals don't value lives.' I was incredulous. And then they showed the little boy holding the picture of his father and he was crying and crying and crying. . . . I must admit I started crying. What's worse was that I was wearing my Army uniform that day. . . . After the film I tried to think of what was the worst war. . . . I don't think there is a 'worse war'. They're all insane."

A young man in R.O.T.C., whose father was a Navy flier, his brother a Navy commander: "My entire semester has been a paradox. I go to your class and I see a Vietnam vet named Joe Bangert tell of his experiences in the war. I was enthralled by his talk. . . . By the end of that hour and a half I hated the Vietnam war as much as he did. The only problem is that three hours after that class I am marching around in my uniform . . . and feeling great about it. . . . Is there something wrong with me? Am I being hypocritical? Sometimes I don't know . . ."

A young woman: "As a white middle class person I've never felt discriminated against at all. But I'll say this: If anyone ever tried to make me sit in a different schoolroom, use a different bathroom, or anything like that, I would knock them right on their ass. . . . Until hearing the black student in class speak I never realized how strong blacks really feel."

A young woman, a junior in liberal arts: "A lot was said in class that my grandparents worked hard and blah blah blah. . . . Believe me, people have worked just as hard as other people's grandparents have and they have nothing at all to show for it. . . . I was once told that 70% of the people on welfare were under the age of sixteen. . . . If 70% of welfare recipients are children, how do we as the great nation we claim to be justify budget cuts?"

Another young woman: "But the people are the last ones that need their rights stated on paper, for if they're abused or injusticed by government or authority, they can act on the injustice directly, which is direct action. . . . It is really government and authority and institutions and corporations that need laws and rights to insulate them from the physicality, the directness of the people."

I found my students, in the supposedly placid eighties, fascinated by the movements of the sixties. It was clear they *longed* to be part of something more inspiring than taking their scheduled places in the American commercial world.

The great popularity of certain readings I assigned told me something about these young people. They were moved by the life story of Malcolm X, by the passionate declamation against war in *Johnny Got His Gun*, by the anarchist-feminist spirit of Emma Goldman in her autobiography *Living My Life*. She represented to them the best of the revolutionary idea: not just to change the world, but to change the way you live, now.

One semester I learned that there were several classical musicians signed up in my course. For the very last class of the semester I stood aside while they sat in chairs up front and played a Mozart quartet. Not a customary finale to a class in political theory, but I wanted the class to understand that politics is pointless if it does nothing to enhance the beauty of our lives. Political discussion can sour you. We needed some music.

In the spring of 1988 I made a sudden decision to quit teaching, after thirty-odd years in Atlanta and Boston and three visiting professorships in Paris. I surprised myself by this, because I love teaching, but I wanted more freedom, to write, to speak to people around the country, to have more time with family and friends.

I would have more opportunities to do things with Roz, who

had stopped doing social work, was playing music and painting. Our daughter and her husband, Myla and Jon Kabat-Zinn, lived in the Boston area and we would be able to spend more time with their children, our grandchildren—Will, Naushon, Serena. Our son Jeff and his wife, Crystal Lewis, were settled in Wellfleet, on Cape Cod, where he was directing and acting with the Wellfleet Harbor Actors Theater. We would be able to pay more attention to his work, while enjoying the magnificent ocean beaches and sea air of the Cape, where we shared a beach house with our old Spelman friends, Pat and Henry West.

I also looked forward to pursuing my interest in writing plays. I had watched all of my family members get into theater. Myla and Roz had acted, in Atlanta and Boston. Jeff had made it his life. When the Vietnam War ended, and I felt some breathing space, I wrote a play about Emma Goldman, the anarchist-feminist who, at the turn of the century, created a sensation all over the United States with her daring ideas.

Emma was first produced in New York, at the Theatre for the New City, and Jeff directed it. I enjoyed the idea that my son and I were working together as equals, but no, he as director was in charge! It was a warm and wonderful collaboration. The play was then staged in Boston, brilliantly directed by Maxine Klein, and both theater critics and audiences were enthusiastic. It ran for eight months, the longest-running show in Boston in 1977. There were more productions, in New York, London, Edinburgh, and then (translated into Japanese) a tour of Japan. I caught the fever of the theatrical world and was never cured.

News of my leaving Boston University seemed to spread; my last class was especially crowded, with people there who were not my students, standing against the wall, sitting in the aisles. I answered questions about my decision, and we had a final discussion about justice, the role of the university, the future of the world.

Then I told them that I was ending the class a half-hour early and explained why. There was a struggle going on between the faculty at the B.U. School of Nursing and the administration, which had decided to close the school down because it was not making enough money, in effect firing the nursing faculty. The nurses were picketing that very day in protest. I was going to join them and I invited my students to come along (Roz had given me that idea the evening before). When I left the class, about a hundred students walked with me. The nurses, desperately needing support, greeted us happily, and we marched up and down together.

It seemed a fitting way to end my teaching career. I had always insisted that a good education was a synthesis of book learning and involvement in social action, that each enriched the other. I wanted my students to know that the accumulation of knowledge, while fascinating in itself, is not sufficient as long as so many people in the world have no opportunity to experience that fascination.

I SPENT THE NEXT SEVERAL YEARS responding to invitations to speak here and there around the country. What I discovered was heartening. In whatever town, large or small, in whatever state of the Union, there was always a cluster of men and women who cared about the sick, the hungry, the victims of racism, the casualties of war, and who were doing *something*, however small, in the hope that the world would change.

Wherever I was—whether Dallas, Texas, or Ada, Oklahoma, or Shreveport, Louisiana, or New Orleans or San Diego or Philadelphia, or Presque Isle, Maine, or Bloomington, Indiana, or Olympia, Washington—I found such people. And beyond the handful of activists there seemed to be hundreds, thousands more who were open to unorthodox ideas.

But they tended not to know of each other's existence, and so, while they persisted, they did so with the desperate patience of Sisyphus endlessly pushing that boulder up the mountain. I tried to tell each group that it was not alone, and that the very people who were disheartened by the absence of a national movement were themselves proof of the potential for such a movement. I suppose I was trying to persuade myself as well as them.

The war in the Persian Gulf against Iraq, in early 1991, was especially discouraging to people who had hoped that the era of large-scale military actions by the United States had ended with Vietnam. The newspapers were reporting that 90 percent of those polled supported President Bush's decision to go to war. The whole country seemed festooned with yellow ribbons in support of the troops in the Gulf. It was not easy to oppose the war while making it clear that we were really supporting the troops in our own way, by wanting to bring them home. In the heated-up atmosphere that seemed impossible to do.

Yet wherever I went I kept being surprised. I was not just speaking to small, self-selected antiwar audiences, but to large assemblies of students at universities, community colleges, and high schools—and my criticism of the war, and of war in general, was being received with vigorous agreement.

I concluded not that the polls were wrong in showing 90 percent support for the war, but that the support was superficial, thin as a balloon, artificially bloated by government propaganda and media collaboration, and that it could be punctured by a few hours of critical inspection.

Arriving at a community college in Texas City, Texas (an oil and chemical town near the Gulf Coast), in the midst of the war, I found the lecture room crowded with perhaps five hundred people, mostly beyond college age—Vietnam veterans, retired workers, women returning to school after raising families. They listened quietly as I spoke about the futility of war and the need to use human ingenuity to find other ways to solve problems of aggression and injustice, and then they gave me a great ovation.

As I spoke, I noticed a man sitting in the back of the lecture hall, a man in his forties, in coat and tie, dark-haired, mustached, and I guessed that he was from somewhere in the Middle East. During the long question-discussion period, he was silent, but when the moderator announced, "Time for one more question," he raised his hand and stood up.

"I am an Iraqi," he began. The room became very quiet. He then told how two years before he had become an American citizen, and that during the citizenship ceremony members of the Daughters of the Confederacy had handed out tiny American flags to the new citizens. "I was very proud. I kept that little flag on my desk at work. Last week I heard on the news that my village in northern Iraq, a place of no military significance, was bombed by American planes. I took the flag from my desk and burned it."

The silence in the room was total. He paused. "I was ashamed of being an American." He paused again. "Until tonight, coming here, and listening to all of you speak out against the war." He sat down. For a moment, no one made a sound, and then the room resounded with applause.

Larry Smith, my host in Texas City, was a faculty member at the college, a lean, bearded Texan who looked like Tom Joad in *The Grapes of Wrath*. He became the object of controversy when a colleague of his accused him of being radical and anti-American, suggesting that the trustees fire him. A meeting was held, at which student after student spoke of Larry Smith as a wonderful teacher, and of how he had broadened their thinking in so many ways.

A woman who had been his student said, "All instructors are like pages in a book and without the unabridged edition we'll never get the whole story." The college president said, "If criticizing our government constitutes being anti-American and pro-Communist . . . I suspect we are all guilty." The Trustees unanimously voted to support Smith.

In the spring of 1992 I was invited to Wilkes-Barre, Pennsylvania. There, in the Wyoming Valley, where the Lackawanna and Susquehanna rivers meet, where just before the Revolution all Indian homes in the valley were burned to ashes at the behest of a land company, were several hundred people of conscience joined in an interfaith council. In that council, feminist groups and disarmament groups worked together, and much of their activity was in aid of people in Central America who were struggling against military governments supported by the United States.

A nun and a priest were my hosts there. The priest, Father Jim Doyle, taught ethics at Kings College in Wilkes-Barre. He had been an Italian translator in prisoner-of-war camps in the second World War, and later was galvanized into political activity by the war in Vietnam.

206 / SCENES AND CHANGES

I left Wilkes-Barre thinking that there must be activists like this in a thousand communities around the nation, ignorant of one another. And if so, were there not enormous possibilities for change?

In Boulder, Colorado, I met the remarkable Sender Garlin. He was eighty-eight years old, an old-time journalist for radical newspapers, a short, thin compression of enormous energy. He had organized my visit and said to me with confidence, "I've been publicizing the meeting. I think at least five hundred people will be there." There were a thousand.

Boulder, it turned out, was alive with all sorts of activity. The local radio station was a mecca of alternative media, airing dissident views all over the Southwest. I met its ace interviewer, David Barsamian, an ingenious impresario of radical broadcasting, who shared his cassettes with a hundred community radio stations around the country.

Going around the country, I was impressed again and again by how favorably people reacted to what, undoubtedly, is a radical view of society—antiwar, anti-military, critical of the legal system, advocating a drastic redistribution of the wealth, supportive of protest even to the point of civil disobedience.

I found this even when speaking to cadets at the Coast Guard Academy in Newport, Rhode Island, or to an assembly of nine hundred students at the reputedly conservative California Polytechnic in San Luis Obispo.

Especially heartening was the fact that wherever I have gone I have found teachers, in elementary school or high school or college, who at some point in their lives were touched by some phenomenon—the civil rights movement, or the Vietnam War, or the feminist movement, or environmental danger, or the plight of peasants in Central America. They were conscientious about teaching their students the practical basics, but also determined to stimulate their students to a heightened social consciousness.

In 1992, teachers all over the country, by the thousands, were beginning to teach the Columbus story in new ways, to recognize that to Native Americans, Columbus and his men were not heroes, but marauders. The point being not just to revise our view of past events, but to be provoked to think about today.

What was most remarkable was that Indian teachers, Indian community activists, were in the forefront of this campaign. How far we have come from that long period of Indian invisibility, when they were presumed to be dead or safely put away on reservations! They have returned, five hundred years after their near annihilation by invading Europeans, to demand that America rethink its beginnings, rethink its values.

It is this change in *consciousness* that encourages me. Granted, racial hatred and sex discrimination are still with us, war and violence still poison our culture, we have a large underclass of poor, desperate people, and there is a hard core of the population content with the way things are, afraid of change.

But if we see only that, we have lost historical perspective, and then it is as if we were born yesterday and we know only the depressing stories in this morning's newspapers, this evening's television reports.

Consider the remarkable transformation, in just a few decades, in people's consciousness of racism, in the bold presence of women demanding their rightful place, in a growing public awareness that homosexuals are not curiosities but sensate human beings, in the long-term growing skepticism about military intervention despite the brief surge of military madness during the Gulf War.

It is that *long-term* change that I think we must see if we are not to lose hope. Pessimism becomes a self-fulfilling prophecy; it reproduces itself by crippling our willingness to act.

There is a tendency to think that what we see in the present moment we will continue to see. We forget how often in this century we have been astonished by the sudden crumbling of institutions, by extraordinary changes in people's thoughts, by unexpected eruptions of rebellion against tyrannies, by the quick collapse of systems of power that seemed invincible.

The bad things that happen are repetitions of bad things that have always happened—war, racism, maltreatment of women, religious and nationalist fanaticism, starvation. The good things that happen are unexpected.

Unexpected, and yet explainable by certain truths which spring at us from time to time, but which we tend to forget:

Political power, however formidable, is more fragile than we think. (Note how nervous are those who hold it.)

Ordinary people can be intimidated for a time, can be fooled for a time, but they have a down-deep common sense, and sooner or later they find a way to challenge the power that oppresses them.

People are not *naturally* violent or cruel or greedy, although they can be made so. Human beings everywhere want the same things: they are moved by the sight of abandoned children, homeless families, the casualties of war; they long for peace, for friendship and affection across lines of race and nationality.

Revolutionary change does not come as one cataclysmic moment (beware of such moments!) but as an endless succession of surprises, moving zig-zag towards a more decent society.

We don't have to engage in grand, heroic actions to participate in the process of change. Small acts, when multiplied by millions of people, can transform the world.

To be hopeful in bad times is not just foolishly romantic. It is based on the fact that human history is a history not only of cruelty, but also of compassion, sacrifice, courage, kindness.

What we choose to emphasize in this complex history will determine our lives. If we see only the worst, it destroys our capacity to do something. If we remember those times and places—and there are so many—where people have behaved magnificently, this gives us the energy to act, and at least the possibility of sending this spinning top of a world in a different direction.

And if we do act, in however small a way, we don't have to wait for some grand utopian future. The future is an infinite succession of presents, and to live *now* as we think human beings should live, in defiance of all that is bad around us, is itself a marvelous victory.

Acknowledgments

I want to thank my Beacon Press editor, Andy Hrycyna, for extraordinarily astute editing, as well as sympathetic support through the whole process. Also Wendy Strothman, director of Beacon Press, for her wise counsel. And Chris Kochansky, who was much more than a copy editor; her quiet suggestions showed a wonderful literary sensibility. Also Rick Balkin, my steadfast literary agent, who prodded me for years to do this and is therefore totally responsible for whatever calamities follow. And Roslyn Zinn, always my first and last reader.

Index